Collins

English for Exams

D0557966

Grammar
for IELTS

Fiona Aish &
Jo Tomlinson

HarperCollins Publishers
77-85 Fulham Palace Road
Hammersmith
London W6 8JB

First edition 2012

Reprint 10 9 8 7 6 5 4 3 2 1 0

© HarperCollins Publishers 2012

ISBN 978-0-00-745683-3

Collins ® is a registered trademark
of HarperCollins Publishers Limited

www.collinselt.com

A catalogue record for this book is available
from the British Library.

Typeset in India by Aptara

Printed in Italy by LEGO SpA, Lavis (Trento)

Contents

Introduction

Who is this book for?

Grammar for IELTS will help improve your grammatical knowledge for all four papers of the IELTS exam. As you know, grammatical accuracy and range are part of the marking criteria for the IELTS Writing and Speaking papers. Also, grammatical accuracy is important in the IELTS Listening and Reading papers. The book can be used for self-study or as supplementary material for IELTS preparation classes. It is suitable for learners at level 5.0-5.5 aiming for band 6.0 or higher.

Summary

The *Grammar for IELTS* book and CD cover grammar and skills which are relevant to all four exam papers: Listening, Reading, Writing and Speaking. Each unit begins with a grammar section presenting the key grammar for the unit with example sentences and explanations. This grammar section is followed by exercises that help you develop the grammatical knowledge and skills needed for the exam. At the end of each unit, there is an exam practice section which is modelled on the actual IELTS exam. Tips throughout the book highlight essential grammar-related learning strategies and exam techniques.

Content

Units

Each unit is divided into three parts.

The first part introduces key grammar using Collins COBUILD grammar explanations and example sentences.

The second part, containing **Practice exercises**, provides a structured set of exercises which help you develop the skills to successfully apply grammatical knowledge to the exam. The exercises are a combination of traditional grammar exercises and exercises based on the IELTS exam.

The third part, containing **Exam practice**, provides exam practice exercises in a format that follows the actual exam giving you the opportunity to familiarize yourself with the kinds of questions you will encounter in the exam. This section focuses on a particular exam paper and is highlighted in grey for easy reference.

Exam tips

There are exam tips and strategies in each unit. These are in boxes for easy reference.

Audio script

All audio for the Listening and Speaking papers has been recorded on the CD using native speakers of English. A full audio script, including model answers for the Speaking papers, is provided at the back of the book so that you can check the language used in the listening and speaking exercises, if needed.

Answer key

A comprehensive answer key is provided for all sections of the book including model answers for more open-ended writing and speaking tasks.

Grammar reference

There is a detailed grammar reference section at the back of the book where the forms of the grammar points presented in the units are provided for your reference. There is a note in the unit telling you which page to refer to in the Grammar reference section.

How to use this book

The book is divided into 20 units. Each unit is self-contained so that you can study the units in any order. You can choose the unit you want to study either by selecting the grammar you want to study or selecting which exam papers you want to practise. A sub-skill is also practised in each unit. As a result, only the units with practice on Speaking and Listening papers contain audio. The contents pages at the beginning of the book provide an overview of what is in each unit so you can use this to choose which units you would like to study first. These pages also give you information on which units contain audio.

You will probably find it helpful to begin each unit by reading the grammar section in the first part, then working through the exercises in preparation for the exam practice exercise at the end. Try to do the exam exercises within the time limit to give yourself realistic exam practice.

Getting well-informed feedback on your writing and speaking exam practice exercises would also be an advantage. However, if this is not possible, it is still important to do the exercises in full. Studying model answers can help you develop the ability to assess your own work. If possible, record yourself when speaking and listen carefully to your performance. Avoid memorizing model answers for the Writing and Speaking papers. Remember that in the actual exam, it is important to answer the question and not just speak or write about the topic.

As part of your final preparation before the exam, you could re-read the exam tips in the boxes. This will remind you of the strategies for success in the exam.

1 Holidays and travel

Simple tenses

Present simple: The present simple is used to talk about:

1 *Permanent situations*

I <u>work</u> in the city but I <u>live</u> in the countryside.	Rome <u>is</u> the capital of Italy.

2 *Things which happen often or repeatedly*

I <u>visit</u> my grandparents in Scotland every summer.	People often <u>send</u> postcards from interesting places.

3 *Facts of nature or science*

Travelling by plane <u>uses</u> a lot of energy.	Birds <u>migrate</u> in winter.

4 *Timetables*

The bus <u>departs</u> at 9.10.	The train to London <u>leaves</u> every 30 minutes.

Past simple: The past simple is used to talk about:

1 *Completed actions or events in the past*

I <u>visited</u> the museums in New York.	I <u>saw</u> some monuments on holiday.

2 *Actions or events that happened at a specific time in the past (when)*

Last month I <u>went</u> on holiday for 2 weeks.	I <u>travelled</u> to Tokyo last year.

3 *Things which happened often or regularly in the past*

We always <u>went</u> on holiday to France when I was a child.	Every summer I <u>spent</u> the school holidays with my cousins.

Present perfect simple: The present perfect simple is used to talk about:

1 *Actions which started in the past and continue now*

I've worked abroad for ten years.	He has lived in Germany since 2002.

2 *Actions in the past when the time is not finished.*

I've visited many art galleries this year. (This year is not finished)	He has lived in a lot of different places in his life. (His life is not finished)

3 *Recent events which are related to the present*

Where's my camera? Oh no, someone has stolen it.	Is Sarah having dinner with us? No, she has gone back to the campsite to rest.

See page 114 in the Grammar reference for more information.

Practice exercises

1 **Decide on the correct tense (present simple, past simple or present perfect simple) and finish the sentences. Decide which rule matches the meaning of each sentence.**

1 The sun often _____ in Morocco. (*shine*) *Tense:* ___Shi___ *Rule number:* ___I___

2 'It's late. Where _you've gone_?' (*you/go*) *Tense:* ___P.P.S___ *Rule number:* ___2___

3 What time _the bus leaves_? (*the bus/leave*) *Tense:* ___P.S.___ *Rule number:* ___IV___

4 John _went_ (*go*) to Finland last year, but he _liked_ (*like*) it. *Tense:* ___Past Simple___
    Rule number: ___1___

5 The world _has seen_ (*see*) a massive shift in transport and tourism in the last decade.
    Tense: ___P.P.S.___ *Rule number:* ___2___

6 Cruise ships _crossed_ (*cross*) the Atlantic with the majority of people before air travel
    became so affordable. *Tense:* ___P.P.S___ *Rule number:* ___III___

> **Exam tip:** Practise listening to and saying the contracted form of some verbs, for
> example: *he has taken = he's taken, I have been = I've been*

2   Below is a section of a candidate answer from an IELTS essay task (Writing Task 2).
     Complete the spaces with the correct tenses.

     "Discuss the positive and negative effects of tourism on people and the environment."

     Regarding the environment, tourism (1) _____ (*improve*) people's understanding of
     endangered species. Prior to mass tourism, many societies (2) _____ (*disregard*)
     the natural life around them. However, due to tourism many countries (3) _____
     have ~~ed~~ (*invest*) in conservation programmes. Ecotourism is now a very popular and a lot of tourists
     (4) ~~have ed~~ (*visit*) Africa, Asia and South America and (5) ~~partake~~ (*partake*) in
     projects which care for the environment. Although there are positive points, tourism
     (6) ~~demad~~ (*also have*) a large number of negative effects on the environment. These
     (7) ~~includes~~ (*include*) an increase in air pollution from plane travel, rubbish from
     tourists in parks and on beaches and the destruction of many of the world's rain forests.

     There are advantages and disadvantages for people too. During the 1990s in many
     parts of the world, *such as* Spain or Thailand, tourism (8) ~~has brought~~ (*bring*) economic   *taught*
     development and (9) ~~has ed~~ (*create*) a range of new employment possibilities for   *bring*
     local people. On the other hand, the results of this increase in tourism sometimes produce
     negative effects for populations. Often a new hotel or resort (10) ~~destroyed~~ (*destroy*)
     traditional jobs such as agriculture, fishing and crafts.

3   Read the following dialogue and complete the text with the correct form of the present
     simple, past simple or present perfect simple. Use the verbs in the brackets.

     Examiner: Where (1) _____ (*live*)?

     Nikolas: I (2) _____ (*come*) from Moscow. I (3) _____ (*live*) there for 6 years. My
     family (4) _____ (*move*) from the countryside when I was 12 years old.

     Examiner: (5) _____ still (6) _____ (*live*) with your family?

     Nikolas: Yes, I (7) _____ (*do*). I (8) _____ (*live*) with my parents and (9) _____ (*share*)
     a room with my brother. My brother still (10) _____ (*go*) to school. He is only 8 years old.

     Examiner: (11) _____ (*like*) Moscow?

     Nikolas: Yes, I (12) _____ (*love*) Moscow. When I first (13) _____ (*arrive*), I (14) _____
     (*not like*) it much because it was so different, but I (15) _____ (*grow*) accustomed to it. Now, I
     (16) _____ (*know*) my way around and (17) _____ (*have*) lots of friends.

     Examiner: How (18) _____ (*Moscow/change*) recently?

     Nikolas: It (19) _____ (*become*) more international, and more exciting. In the last few
     years, about ten new international restaurants (20) _____ (*open*) in my area alone
     and I often (21) _____ (*eat*) in them now with my friends. I (22) _____ (*have*) lots of
     international friends who (23) _____ (*come*) to study at the University in Moscow, and
     we often (24) _____ (*meet*) in the evenings.

01

Now listen and check your answers to Exercise 3.

> **Speaking exam tip:** Try to answer the question the examiner asks you, and give more information. Nikolas has talked about a change and then the result of that change.

4 **Answer these questions yourself and try to give as much information as possible.**

1 Where do you live? _____

2 How long have you lived there? _____

3 What do you like about your home town? _____

4 What other countries have you visited? _____

5 Where did you go on holiday last year? _____

6 How often do you go to the seaside? _____

Exam practice: Speaking Part 1

02

Listen to the 5 questions on the CD, and answer them as fully as possible. You will have 30 seconds between questions to give your answers.

> **Speaking exam tip:** Try to mirror the examiner's grammar in the first sentence of your answer and use the contracted form in your answer where you can, e.g. 'Have you lived...?' – 'I've lived....' 'Do you like...?' – 'I like...'

03

Now listen to Track 03 on the CD and the model answers given by the student. How were they better than or different from your answers?

_____

_____

_____

_____

_____

_____

_____

2   Free time

Continuous tenses

The continuous tenses highlight the duration of the activity so that there is a focus on the activity in progress.

Present continuous: The present continuous is used to talk about:

1 *Something that is happening / in progress now*

> Some people <u>are sitting</u> on the grass and <u>having</u> a picnic.

2 *Changes and developments*

> The number of Web users who shop online <u>is increasing</u>.

3 *Temporary situations*

> My friend <u>is staying</u> in a holiday camp.

Past continuous: The past continuous is used to talk about:

1 *Continuing past actions happening at the same time as another event.*

> I <u>was swimming</u> in the sea when the rain started.

2 *Describing situations in the past*

> Some people <u>were relaxing</u> by the pool and others <u>were playing</u> tennis.

3 *Temporary situations in the past*

> For the first two days of my holiday I <u>was staying</u> with friends.

Present perfect continuous: The present perfect continuous is used to talk about:

1 *Actions that started in the past and are continuing now*

> My best friend <u>has been learning</u> French since January.

2 *When you mention the results of a recent activity*

I'm so tired. I've been waiting for the train for hours.

3 *When we want to emphasize the repetition or duration of an action*

They've been thinking about where to go this weekend.

See page 115 in the Grammar reference for more information.

Practice exercises

1   Decide on the correct tense (present continuous, past continuous or present perfect continuous) and complete the sentences 1–6 using the verbs in the brackets. Decide which rule matches the meaning of each sentence.

 1 'What _____ (*do*)?' You look exhausted!'
 Tense: _____ Rule number: _____

 2 'Can you help me with my homework?' 'No, I _____ TV.' (*watch*)
 Tense: _____ Rule number: _____

 3 The number of people taking up extreme sports _____ (*increase*) since the early 1990s.
 Tense: _____ Rule number: _____

 4 Last month I _____ (*have*) acting lessons but I had to stop when I lost my voice.
 Tense: _____ Rule number: _____

 5 They _____ (*walk*) in the countryside when suddenly it started to rain.
 Tense: _____ Rule number: _____

 6 I don't like the book that I _____ (*read*) at the moment.
 Tense: _____ Rule number: _____

> **Grammar tip:** Continuous verbs are usually **active** verbs (verbs such as *to run*), that refer to an action). **Stative** verbs (such as *to know*), refer to a state, and are usually used in simple tenses, e.g. *I want a new bike* not *I am wanting a new bike* as *to want* is a state, not an action.
>
> Some verbs such as *to see* have both an active and a stative meaning.

2   Look at the following sentences 1–5 and decide if the main verbs should be in the present continuous or the present simple.

 1 *I am not agreeing / I don't agree* that going to the cinema is better than watching films on TV.
 2 *I have / I am having* a great time in Paris at the moment. (meaning = to enjoy)
 3 *I like / I am liking* studying Spanish in my free time.
 4 *Do you mind / Are you minding* if I sit here?
 5 *I think / I'm thinking* about learning to sail next year. (meaning = to plan to do)

3 Underline the examples of continuous tenses in the following passage from a Reading text, then complete the summary below using continuous verbs from the text.

The amount of leisure time available to people has been increasing since the early twentieth century when machines started to be invented to do many labour intensive tasks both at work and in the home. Previously, people were spending many more hours doing basic menial tasks and as a result had less time available for hobbies and activities. Although recently many people have been complaining about their work life balance, studies show that the amount of free time we have has been rising continuously for over 50 years. More people are playing sport on a regular basis nowadays and young people are taking up traditional style hobbies such as knitting and walking in the countryside. There has also been a large amount of government investment in leisure facilities in local communities, which has assisted the uptake of hobbies for a range of people including children and the elderly. A few years ago, visitors to a local park would see people who were playing football or walking their dog. However, nowadays people are using the gym or a climbing wall as their way of sporting recreation.

Summary

Over the last half century the amount of personal free time that people have
(1) _____. Despite the fact that the general opinion of the public is that they have less leisure time than in the past the reality is the opposite. Nowadays more of us
(2) _____ sport regularly and the younger generation (3) _____ traditional leisure pursuits such as crafts and outdoor activities.

4 Look at the graphs below from an IELTS Writing Task 1 and complete the sentences with the correct tense to describe the visual information.

a Number of people buying newspapers daily in the USA

Overall, the number of people who buy one of the three major daily newspapers in the USA (1) _____ (rising) since the 1950s. The largest increase in readership has been for the New York Times. However, most people (2) _____ (still buy) the Washington Post more than any other daily newspaper.

b Viewers of UK TV channels at 8 p.m. on 30 June 2011

The graph shows the number of people who (1) _____ (view) four different television channels on 30 June 2011 at 8.00 in the evening. Almost half the viewers (2) _____ (watch) BBC1 and the remaining 50 per cent were divided more or less equally between the other three channels.

Exam practice: Writing Task 1

You should spend about 20 minutes on this task.

The graph below shows how elderly people in Europe spent their free time between 1980 and 2010.

Summarize the information by selecting and reporting the main features, and make comparisons where relevant.

Write at least 150 words.

> **Writing exam tip:** When describing visual information in Task 1, it is important to think about what tenses you will need. If the diagram includes time references (dates, years) you will need a range of past and present tenses. If the graph has no past time reference, you will need to use the present simple tense only.

Free time activities of the elderly in Europe from 1980 to the present

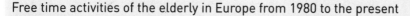

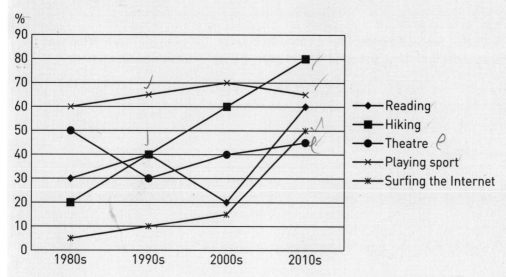

Now compare your answer with the model answer and think about how you could improve yours.

3 Fame

The following forms are used to talk about the past in addition to the past simple tense.

Past perfect: The past perfect is used to talk about:

One completed action that happened before another action in the past. The past perfect is used for the first action

Before he became the 2010 world swimming champion <u>nobody had heard</u> of James Collins.	Every newspaper and TV channel in the USA wanted to interview Neil Armstrong after <u>he had landed</u> on the moon.

Past perfect continuous: The past perfect continuous is used to talk about:

Something that started in the past and continued up to a certain point in the past

The journalists <u>had been waiting</u> for over an hour by the time the President arrived at the palace.	The Beatles <u>had been playing</u> together for years before they became famous.

Used to: *Used to* is used to talk about:

Past states and habits

The Spanish Royal family <u>used to be</u> more removed from public life than they are at present.	Dickinson <u>used to work</u> in a department store before he became the owner of a fashion chain in Australia.

Note: In the negative and question form, *used to* becomes *use to*.

Would: *Would* is used to talk about:

*The typical activities of a person or people in the past. It should be used for repeated actions and **not** state and is almost always used in the **positive form only***

In the 1930s Hollywood stars <u>would give</u> regular interviews in magazines and newspapers to promote new movies.	Before publishing companies, writers <u>would often pay</u> for their own printing and distribution costs.

See page 116 in the Grammar reference for more information.

Practice exercises

1   Complete the sentences 1–6 using the verbs in the brackets and decide on the correct grammatical form from the alternatives given.

1   Managing an actor's image though media relations become popular in the 1980s. Up until then actors _____ (*not care*) much about their public image.
Form: past perfect or *would*?

2   Newspapers and magazines _____ (*respect*) the privacy of celebrities more than they do nowadays.
Form: used to or past perfect?

3   As a child I loved playing the guitar and I _____ (*dream*) of being a well-known musician.
Form: would or past perfect?

4   Until the 1990s, footballers _____ (*not earn*) such large salaries and they didn't use to be so famous.
Form: past perfect or *would*?

5   Before working in television I _____ (*always think*) that celebrities were special people, but now I know many of them are quite normal.
Form: past perfect or past perfect continuous?

6   The photographers _____ (*wait*) hours for the stars to arrive at the 2010 Oscar ceremony.
Form: past perfect continuous or *used to*?

> **Grammar tip:** The past perfect is often used with a time expression such as *before*, *when* or *by the time*.
>
> Unlike the present perfect, specific times (e.g. *in 1993*) can be used with the past perfect.

2   Listen to a radio programme about fame and complete the text with the correct verb forms.
04

In today's programme I'll continue examining the impact of fame on lifestyle using the style icon Gloria Van Broncken as an example. Before becoming famous in the modelling industry, Gloria (1) _____lived_____ in a small village and (2) _____ outside her own country. She (3) _____worked_____ in a clothes store and she enjoyed all the usual activities of a teenager in her free time. She (4) _____ in the clothes store for two years when a customer who represented a model agency spotted her and signed her up. By the time she was 21 Gloria (5) _____had travelled_____ round the world several times and (6) _____ on the cover of many international fashion magazines. Now the impact of such drastic lifestyle changes can be very significant ... (*fade*)

3 Read the following text about a famous businesswoman and correct the mistakes in the use of past perfect, past perfect continuous, *used* to and *would*. There are four mistakes.

Making money out of other people's fame is a highly specialised skill, but one that can bring great rewards to those who practise it proficiently. Marianne Beretoli is one of those people; she owns a company which sells information about celebrities to other celebrities as a kind of careers advice service. Although she was born in France, she use to dream of moving to the USA, specifically Hollywood. Whilst studying business at university Beretoli was known for her innovative approach to applying theory to practice and she would to often challenge the ideas of her tutors. When she had graduated, Beretoli worked in Paris and tried unsuccessfully to set up her own marketing agency. Then she decided to move to the USA and within months realised that she had been making the right decision. She moved from Paris to Los Angeles in 1995 and after she had been working as an assistant for an advertising agency for a few years, she had set up her own company providing information services to the rich and famous.

4 Read the text again and the multiple-choice questions below. Decide which answer A–D is correct.

1 Marianne Beretoli moved to the USA...

    A immediately after she had graduated from university.

    B after she had tried to start her own company and not been successful.

    C after she had been working for an agency in the advertising field for several years.

    D before she studied business.

2 How did Beretoli behave while studying business at university?

    A She used to be a challenge.

    B She would challenge the relationship between theory and practice.

    C She would question her lecturers' ideas.

    D She ignored the advice of her tutors.

> **Exam Tip:** It is not usual for the Reading exam to test your knowledge of tenses directly. However, having a good understanding of tenses will help you understand a text more thoroughly and quickly.

Exam practice: Reading – multiple-choice questions

Look at the passage below.
For question 1, choose TWO letters A–E.
For questions 2 and 3, choose ONE answer from the letters a–d.

1 What reasons do scientists give to explain why some people may want to be famous?

   A Because they didn't have many friends when they were children.

   B They want to copy celebrities they see in the media.

   C They did not receive enough attention from their parents in their youth.

   D So that they can be rich in the future.

   E They had a desire to please their parents.

2 What did the scientists do in order to reach their conclusions?

   a They analysed the increase in celebrity news in the media.

   b They surveyed culturally diverse sections of population.

   c They investigated different universities.

   d They interviewed psychologists.

3 In the study, how were the people who want to be rich different from those who want to be famous?

   a Their parents helped them to be successful.

   b People close to them had urged them to do well.

   c They measured their success by focusing on the future.

   d Their parents taught them about business.

The Psychology of Fame

Until the beginning of the 1990s western psychologists had not systematically studied the human desire to be famous. However, in the few years up to this time the amount of celebrity news in the media had been increasing dramatically. Scientists at various US universities then started to investigate the reasons why some humans seem to be driven to become famous, while others have no interest in attracting the limelight. Extensive research with people from different cultures led to the conclusion that people who desire fame are not the same people who want to be rich. The former group may have some desire for social acceptance based on previous experiences in their lives. It seems that many of these people used to find it difficult to make friends when they were younger or they didn't use to receive praise or recognition from their parents. The psychologists believe that it is likely that these people would often demand attention from others as teenagers and this desire has remained in adulthood and is now expressed as a longing to be famous. Conversely, those who want to be rich are much more focused on the future than the past; in contrast to the former group, the study found that many of this group had learned from their parents that success is generated by hard work and that their friends and family had always encouraged them to strive for the best in life. These conclusions suggest that there is a link between our upbringing and how we measure our success.

4 Education

Future forms

Going to: *Going to* is used to talk about:

1 *A decided plan or intention*

I <u>am going to ask</u> you some questions.	The headmaster <u>is going to retire</u> at the end of term.

2 *A prediction based on evidence*

The shortage of maths teachers <u>is going to get</u> worse.	My grades have gone down this year. I think I'm <u>going to fail</u>.

Will: *Will* is used to talk about:

1 *Facts about the future*

We <u>will cover</u> this topic in more detail later in the book.	The university <u>will admit</u> five hundred more students next year.

2 *Decisions about the future that we make at the moment of speaking*

I'<u>ll try</u> my best to answer all the questions.	'I need to go to the library later.' – 'Good idea. I'<u>ll come</u> with you.'

3 *Predictions that are indefinite*

Online learning <u>will become</u> more popular in the future.	All large libraries <u>will want</u> a copy of this book.

4 *Promises and offers*

I'<u>ll deal</u> with your question in just a moment.

*Note: Shall is usually used in place of *will* in the question form.*

<u>Shall</u> we start again from the beginning?

Won't: *Won't* is the negative of *will* and it is also used to talk about:

Refusal

The teachers say they <u>won't</u> attend meetings out of school hours.

See page 117 in the Grammar reference for more information.

Practice exercises

1 Decide on the correct grammatical form (*will* or *going to*) and complete the sentences 1–5. Decide which rule matches the meaning of each sentence.

    1 'I've made a revision timetable for the next month. I _____ study hard for this exam!' *Form:* _____ *Rule:* _____

    2 'In the future, I think more people _____will_____ study courses online.' *Form:* _____ *Rule:* _____

    3 'Alejandro has failed many of his exams, so I don't think he _____ be able to go to University this year.' *Form:* _____ *Rule:* _____

    4 'No I _____won't_____ let you borrow my calculator. I need it for the next exercise.' *Form:* _____

    5 The next academic year _____will_____ start in September. *Form:* _____ *Rule:* _____

> **Grammar tip:** *Going to* and *will* are based on perspective when used for predictions, and can often be interchangeable. Sometimes, when a person uses *will* they are not so sure. When a person uses *going to* they are surer. However, as perspectives are subjective, there is not usually one correct answer.
>
> *I'll go to one of the best universities in the country.* (this prediction is probably based on what the speaker wants and hopes)
>
> *I'm going to go to one of the best universities in the country.* (this prediction is more likely to be based on the student's knowledge of their own academic achievement, for example, if they always get the top grades in their class)

2 Read the answers A–C to this Part 3 Speaking exercise and match them to the questions 1–3.

    1 How do you think education will change in the future?

    2 What are the main arguments about education in your country at the moment?

    3 Do you think education will be accessible to all in future?

A. Well, the government **is going to** introduce compulsory tuition fees next academic year, and this has caused a lot of anger. Students have been protesting about the unfairness of these fees. They think that poorer students **won't** be able to afford the fees. The government **won't** back down though.

B. In one way, yes. I think more people **will** be able to access basic education around the world, like primary and secondary schools, and also courses online in practical subjects. But I think university education **will** become more exclusive. I read an article recently about how the Internet **is going to** make education available for the world, but I think that **will** mean that good university degrees will be more important.

C. I think a lot of people **will** study online. The Internet **is going to** be easily accessible in all countries soon and online courses are cheaper and more convenient than having to travel to a college or campus. I also think more and more people **will** be able to study.

Look again at the questions in Exercise 2 and think about how *you* would answer them using *will* and *going to*.

> **Listening exam tip:** In the Listening exam, people sometimes contradict each other to distract from the correct answer. For example:
>
> *John: I'm going to be at home later, so I can do some research on the Internet.*
> *Bill: No, I'll do it. There are computers I can use at the library.* (Instant decision)
>
> Here we can see that Bill offers to do the Internet research, although John first mentions it.

3 **Look at these sentences 1–3 and write answers that contradict them. Use the verbs in the brackets.**

1 **Alex:** I'll pick you up from school later if you would like.

Paula: No, that's okay. I _____ (*walk*) home as I want to get some sweets from the shop. (Plan)

2 **Philip:** I'm going to see Jane tonight, so I can tell her about the homework.

Fiona: Don't worry, I _____ (*call*) her, as I want to speak to her anyway. (Instant decision)

3 **Mike:** I'm going to walk over to the library tonight and take my book back.

Penny: _____ (*do*) it? It's easy for me to drive down. (Offer)

Mike: Thanks!

4 **Look at the audio script below and correct any mistakes in the future forms. There are five mistakes.**

Librarian: Hello there. How can I help you?
John: I will do a presentation on Mary Shelley, and I'd like to get some books on her.
Librarian: Okay. The biographies are on the third floor. I'll to write the aisle number down for you.
John: Thanks. I might use the Internet too and look for resources on there.
Librarian: That's a good idea. If you're going use the Internet, have a look on the Great British Authors website.
John: Thanks, I'm going to. I haven't heard of that site before. Thanks very much for the information.
Librarian: That's quite all right. Feel free to come and ask me any questions and I won't do my best to help.

Listen to Track 05 on the CD and check your answers.

Exam practice: Listening Section 1 – classifying

> **Listening exam tip:** Classifying questions ask you to choose items from a list of options. Sometimes you have more options than needed (see Q1–3 below) and sometimes you must reuse options (see Q4–8 below).

Listen to the discussion between a new student and someone in the Student Affairs Office and answer questions **1–8** below:

06

Who does what?
Write the correct letter **A, B, C, D** or **E** next to questions **1–3**.

1 Andy _____

2 Carol _____

3 Administration Office _____

    A completes the New Student Form.

    B books the library induction.

    C stamps the paperwork.

    D finds the campus map.

    E pays the student fees.

Where should Andy go for the following things?
Write the correct letter **A, B** or **C** next to questions **4–8**.

4 Flat rentals _____

5 Tenancy agreement information _____

6 Doctor registration _____

7 Local area information _____

8 Course fee payment _____

    A Student Support Service

    B Administrative Department

    C Student Affairs

5   The Internet

Other future forms

Present continuous: The present continuous is used to talk about:

Definite arrangements in the future (with active verbs)

I'm meeting John later this afternoon.	I'm playing a computer game with him later.

Future continuous: The future continuous is used to talk about:

A situation that will be happening at a particular point in the future

This time next year, most people will be using the Internet every day.	Tomorrow afternoon, I'll be building my new website.

Future perfect simple: The future perfect simple is used to talk about:

Something that happens before a certain point of time in the future

Everyone will have learnt how to use the Internet in 50 years' time.	I will have spent over £200 on online shopping by the end of the week!

Future perfect continuous: The future perfect continuous is used to talk about:

Something that continues until a certain point of time in the future

Next month, I will have been working at this Internet design company for ten years.	Come on, it's my turn! Soon you will have been surfing the net for over two hours.

Note: The future continuous, future perfect simple and future perfect continuous usually include a time reference, for example *by 2020, in 20 years' time, by this time next year, next week.*

See page 118 in the Grammar reference for more information.

Practice exercises

1 Decide on the correct grammatical form (present continuous, future continuous, future perfect simple or future perfect continuous) and complete the sentences 1–5. Use the verbs in the brackets. Then write the name of the tense.

1 I _will have been watching_ (watch) the concert live online tonight. Tense: _____

2 Media experts predict that by 2020 the majority of newspapers _will have become be_ (move) online. Tense: _____

3 I _am changing_ (change) my Internet supplier tonight so I might not get your emails until tomorrow. Tense: _____

4 The Internet _will have become_ (become) the primary source of information by the middle of the century. Tense: _____

5 It is estimated that in five years' time 30% more people over the age of 65 _will have started_ (start) to use the Internet. Tense: _____

2 Underline the examples of the future forms in the following text.

The Rise of Online Shopping

In the late 1990s experts predicted that online shopping would not be able to compete with in-store shopping yet the recent rise in online sales figures suggests that their predictions were wrong. In fact all evidence points to the fact that online shopping will have outstripped in-store shopping within the next five years. This rapid increase has been driven by a number of factors including price, convenience and choice. Most online retailers use a delivery service and as a result of tracking retailers shopping habits, many will soon be introducing specific delivery timings so that customers can ensure their goods are delivered when they are at home. Online companies are already working on innovative ways to attract customers. For example, later this year one of the country's largest electronics retailers, Browns, is launching a 24-hour replacement products service for customers who need to return faulty goods. Browns hopes that by 2015 over 90% of its customer base will have graduated to online purchasing.

As well as consumer goods another growth area is the travel industry. Travel experts estimate that in as little as five years' time travel agencies will have disappeared from our shopping centres and almost all travellers will be buying hotels and flights from online agencies.

3 Look at the previous text again and match the sentence halves below using the grammatical forms to help you understand when the actions happen.

1 Browns will be   *c*

2 In 5 years, travel agencies will have   *E*

3 Browns claims that by 2015 customers will have   *A*

4 In the future the majority of customers will be   *B*

5 In 5 years' time, shopping on computers will have   *D*

A moved to online shopping. *e*

B shopping online for holidays.

C launching a returns service. *1*

D overtaken physical shopping.

E disappeared from shopping centres. *e*

4 Listen to an interview about online gaming and complete spaces 1–4 in the table with information from the recording. Remember that the answers will be factual information but the grammar forms will help you decide what information is needed.

Online gaming trends of the future

Year	now – 2015	2015 – 2017	2018 – 2020
Age group	13 – 19	30 – 40	**1** over 5 0s
Game type	platform	**2** network games	3D
World region	**3** Asra	Eastern Europe	worldwide
Competition	none	**4** _____	unknown

5 Listen to the interview again and complete sentences 1–4 below with the correct future form.

1 By 2020 the typical age of gamers _____ to people over the age of 50.

2 The over 50s age group _____ the same games for more than 50% of their lives by 2020.

3 Companies that make computer games _____ a global marketing system for every game they produce by 2020.

4 By 2015 technology firms _____ the technology needed to enable people to interact with movies.

Exam practice: Listening – completing a table

Exam tip: Remember that in the IELTS Listening exam you may hear the contracted form of a verb, e.g. *it'll've started* rather than *it will have started*.

08

Listen to a museum curator talking about three exhibitions on technology and complete the table below.

QUESTIONS 1–6

Write **NO MORE THAN THREE WORDS OR A NUMBER** for each answer.

Where	1 _first_ floor	third floor	fourth floor
Exhibition name	The Internet: Past, Present and Future	3 _Social_ Networking	Portable Devices of the 21st Century
Exhibition dates	2 July _31_	August 1st – 30th	5 _July 22nd_ – August 20th
What to see	3D touch screens	4 world _____	6 sixth sense technology and satellite _tracking systems_

6 The family

Basic word order

Word order is important in English. Sentences usually follow the principle:

Subject + Verb + Object/Complement + Further information

My brother kicked the ball.	Roles within the family are becoming flexible in modern society.
Subject = *brother* Verb = *kick* Object = *ball*	Subject = *Roles within the family* Verb = *are becoming*; Adjective = *flexible* Prepositional phrase = *in modern society*

The indirect object:

Without *to*: S + V + <u>Indirect object</u> + Object

The 1912 law gave women the right to vote.

With *to*:   S + V + Object + *to* + <u>Indirect object</u>

The 1912 law gave the right to vote <u>to women</u>.

Time and place phrases:

<u>(Time)</u> + Subject + Verb +(Object) + <u>Place</u> + <u>(Time)</u>

<u>In the twentieth century</u>, more women went out to work <u>in offices</u>.
OR
More women went out to work <u>in offices</u> <u>in the twentieth century</u>.

Common word positioning:

Adjective + Noun	He comes from a <u>large family</u>.
Adverb + Main verb	The siblings <u>continually argue</u>. They <u>have always argued</u>.
Adverb + Adjective	Family structures can be <u>extremely complex</u>.

Note: enough is an exception

Adverbs can be found at the front of a sentence when making a comment on the sentence or linking a previous sentence. There are many exceptions to adverb position, particularly in speaking.

Note: Adverbs often go after the verb *to be*, e.g. *My brother <u>is often</u> annoying*.

Subject and object questions:

Questions are formed differently depending on whether the question is about the subject or the object.

The nuclear family overtook the extended family in popularity.

About the subject: What overtook the extended family in popularity? (Question word + Verb + Object/Compliment?)	*Answer:* The nuclear family.
About the object: What did the nuclear family overtake in popularity? (Question word + Auxiliary verb + Subject + Main verb?)	*Answer:* The extended family.

Indirect questions:

Indirect questions are formed using the word order of a positive sentence.

DIRECT:	*What did the nuclear family overtake in popularity?*
INDIRECT:	*Do you know what the nuclear family overtook in popularity?*
DIRECT:	*Are the roles of husband and wife less traditional than in the past?*
INDIRECT:	*Can you tell me if the roles of husband and wife are less traditional than in the past?*

The Basic Rules of Punctuation:

Capital letter (A) Used: at the start of a sentence; for names; for abbreviations.

Comma (,) Used: for lists of items; to join two clauses together with a co-ordinating conjunction; to show extra information in a sentence; to separate direct speech from reporting expressions.

Full Stop (.) Used: at the end of a sentence and for some abbreviations, e.g. *etc.*; for questions, replace a full stop with a question mark; for exclamations, replace a full stop with an exclamation mark.

Quotation marks (" ") Used: when using the direct words of another person.

Apostrophe (') Used: in contractions and to show possessive. Note: *Its* (=belonging to it) and *it's* (=it is).

Colon (:) Used: to start a grammatically complex list and before long explanations.

Semi-Colon (;) Used: to separate a grammatically complex list; to separate two sentences which have a clear link to each other.

Practice exercises

1   Put the words in the correct order to complete the sentences 1–7.

   1 / The male / the main income earner / was / in the last century /

   2 / are / extended families / Do you know / traditional in Japan? / whether /

   3 / gives / benefits / poorer families / The government /

   4 / always / don't / get on well / Family members /

   5 / by men and women / Household tasks / often / shared / are /

   6 / are / Single parent families / becoming / in Western society / increasingly / common /

   7 / There / the family structure / is less important / urgently / on why / need to be studies /

2 Add the punctuation to the following passage.

how important is the family

It it could be argued that the family is a structure in decline, yet many sociologists now claim that we are beginning to see a renewal in family values and family structures jason lloyd an eminent sociologist at the university of salford claims that today people are yearning for the days of traditional family values he asserts ... we can see examples of a renaissance of family values everywhere in the tv adverts that sell products using happy families in the promotions of seasonal family celebrations like christmas even in the language of politicians about social cohesion lloyds claims have recently been echoed by other sociologists around the globe which gives them even more weight so are we beginning to see a return to the traditional family structure only time will tell

09

3 The following Speaking long turn has some mistakes in the word order. Correct the mistakes and then listen and check. There are eight errors.

> *Describe a member of your extended family who is important to you. You should say:*
> - *What they are like*
> - *How often you see them*
> - *Why they are particularly important to you*
>
> *And say in what ways you would like to be similar to them.*

I'm going to talk about my grandmother on my father's side. She is little quite and has white hair and glasses. I have glasses too. We are the only people in the family that wear glasses! She is very old now and I don't get to see her very often ... I think I maybe two or three times a year see her. She lives quite far away in the countryside. It takes us about three hours to travel there. Whenever we visit, she always gives to me sweets. She is important to me because she is so kind and so nice, and really I love her. She is my favourite family member definitely! I think I take after her in some ways. We laugh at the same things and we both like reading. When we go and visit, always we go out walking in the fields and have a really lovely time. My dad always says that we are very similar. I would like to be when I am older as wise as her. I would also like to have a similar life. A very successful career she had. She was a doctor and worked for charities. She was very much in love with my grandfather, which I think is lovely.

> **Exam tip:** Always allow time to edit your work, especially in the Writing exam. Noticing and correcting details like punctuation and word order (as well as spelling and grammatical structure) can improve your score dramatically.

4 Correct the mistakes in the word order and punctuation in the following sample essay.

"Rich and famous people are increasingly adopting children from developing countries. This has overwhelmingly negative effects." Do you agree with this statement? Why?

Adoption has long been a common thing yet there a recent trend has been in adopting children from overseas. This trend has been noted in the media as more and more celebrities have adopted children from other countries. Some people think this is a negative thing, but I think that on the whole the effects positive of this outweigh any negative repercussions as I shall go on to show.

Firstly, adopting from other countries raises the awareness of a countrys plight. Seeing famous people adopting children from countries like cambodia means that cambodia is in the news more and people can find out what there is going on. Also, these children move to richer countries and can tell people about their native country raising awareness on a smaller scale.

Secondly, these children may well not be adopted unless people come from overseas to do it. A happy life in another country is surely better than an unhappy life in the country where a person was born. The new country will give more opportunity the child and a family that they may not get if they were to stay in the orphanage

However for the children to retain their culture it is important. There is a danger that this might not happen if they move to another country. Therefore there should be a rule that the adoptive parents allow the child to revisit their home country and retain their original culture.

In conclusion, I think the personal adoption benefits gives a child and the awareness that can be raised from these adoptions far outweighs any negative factors, such as change of culture.

Exam practice: Writing Task 2

You should spend about 40 minutes on this task.

> **Exam tip:** Manage your time effectively in the Writing exam. For the essay you will have 40 minutes to write, so give yourself time to plan before you begin writing, and try to allow five minutes at the end to read through your work and check for errors.

Write about the following topic:

"The education you receive from your family is more important than the education you receive from school." To what extent do you agree with this statement and why?

Give reasons for your answer and include any relevant examples from your knowledge or experience.

Write at least 250 words.

There is a model answer in the answer key.

7 The environment

Subject + verb agreement:

1 Uncountable nouns take singular verbs.

2 We use groups of people (*the government*, *the team*) + singular OR plural verbs.

Clouds form when water molecules evaporate into the air.	The government is/are building wind farms in the north of the country.

This/that, these/those

1 We use *this/that* + singular nouns and verbs. We use *these/those* + plural nouns and verbs.

2 We use *this/that* and *these/those* to refer back to objects already mentioned. They must agree with the noun already mentioned.

Tropical climates produce great biodiversity. These conditions are found mainly near the equator.

In my opinion this government's record on protecting wildlife is not good enough.

Both/either/neither as a subject

1 We use *both... and...* + plural verbs.

2 We use *either... or...* and *neither... nor...* + singular or plural verbs. The verb form agrees with the second noun.

Both wind power and solar power are alternative forms of energy.	Either the government or the car manufacturers need to make carbon emission reduction their priority.

Each, every, all

1 We use *each* and *every* + singular noun and verb.

2 We use *all* + plural nouns and verbs.

All forms of energy cause some damage to the environment.	Each/every country has to agree on the climate change penalties for oil companies.

Quantifying expressions: *The* + general noun + *of* + specific noun. The verb agrees with the general noun NOT the specific noun.

The <u>amount</u> of pollution <u>has</u> increased dramatically.	The <u>number</u> of pesticides in farming <u>is</u> declining.
The <u>types</u> of pollution <u>are</u> more varied now compared with the 19th century.	The <u>quantities</u> of chemicals in rivers <u>have</u> changed according to environmentalists.

> **Exam tip:** It is important to make sure you check subject + verb agreement in your writing for Tasks 1 and 2. Mistakes in subject + verb agreement will reduce your writing score so you should leave time to check your work and make any necessary corrections in the exam.

Practice exercises

1 **Decide on the correct form (singular or plural) of the verbs in brackets and complete the sentences 1–6.**

   1 Scientists at Oxford University _____ (*believe*) that there are many different solutions to the world's environmental problems.
   2 Sunshine and water _____ (*be*) both necessary for the growth of plants.
   3 This new method of breeding disease resistant crops _____ (*have*) been very successful.
   4 The frequency of storms on the west coast of South America _____ (*change*) with the movement of the Gulf Stream.
   5 The varieties of tomato available as a result of genetically modified food processing _____ (*be*) numerous.
   6 In my opinion all these conferences _____ (*do*) not help solve the issues of climate change.

2 **Match the sentence halves in boxes A and B so that the subjects and verbs agree and the sentences are meaningful. You must make sure the sentence halves agree grammatically as well as in meaning.**

A	B
1 A vast sum of money	a were spent on developing the wind turbines.
2 Both time and money	b is increasing the cost of electricity and gas for consumers.
3 Those energy companies	c was spent on developing the wind turbines.
4 Every energy company in the EU	d are increasing the cost of electricity and gas for consumers.

3   Look at the following graph and correct seven subject + verb mistakes in the text below it.

Number of birds, butterflies and insects in UK city gardens

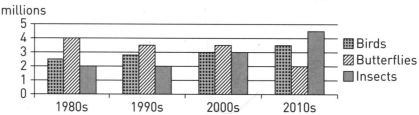

The graph show the amount of wildlife in gardens in cities in the UK from the 1980s to 2010s. Overall, the number of birds and insects have increased, whereas the number of butterflies has decreased. There were four million butterflies in UK city gardens in the 1980s. However, these number decreased rapidly from 2000 to 2010 and now butterflies is the least populous of the three groups with only two million in UK city gardens. Both birds and insects have increased steadily in quantity over the period. The quantity of birds have increased from 2.5 to 3.5 million and insects has increased from 2.0 to 4.5 million. In general it can be said that each decade have seen a rise in bird and insect numbers.

Grammar tip: When you have to complete sentences, remember that the words you write in the spaces must fit grammatically. Check for agreement between nouns and verbs.

4   Complete the sentences 1–4 with words from the following text.

The problem with climate change

In general scientists agree that climate change is happening. However, the point that they disagree on is the speed at which it is happening. For example, Professor Jenkins and Dr Brody at Colombia University think that we are entering a period of rapid climate change, whereas some climatologists from UCLA are of the opinion that the speed of climate change is likely to peak by 2020 and then slow down for the remainder of the 21st century as emissions from developing nations stabilise. The fact that each group of scientists has a different opinion is difficult for people to comprehend and has an effect on the general public's reactions to changes in the law related to climate change. Both governments and scientists have tried to make the information on climate change accessible to everyone but because of its complexity this has not been possible.

1   Neither Professor Jenkins nor Dr Brody _____ that climate change is slowing down.

2   _____ have the view that climate change will speed up over the next few years.

3   Difference of opinion _____ for the general public to understand.

4   Due to the fact that climate change data is complex, the _____ have not been able to make climate change data accessible to people.

> **Exam tip:** Always double check the nouns and verbs in your answers. If you write a singular noun where the answer is plural, your answer will be marked incorrect.

Exam practice: Reading – completing sentences

Read the following passage and answer the questions below, using only words from the text.

Ocean biodiversity

Both the levels of fish stocks and mammal biodiversity in the world's oceans have been declining in recent years as a result of overfishing and marine pollution. Yet new equipment and a return to more traditional ways of fishing have shown how this trend can be reversed. An example of this can be seen in the south Pacific where tuna fishermen have started to use deep sea nets to trawl the depths of the oceans in order to avoid catching and killing smaller fish. The amount of small fish caught with these nets has already been reduced in the south Pacific and fishermen in other oceans across the world are interested in exploring different techniques to minimize their impact on ocean biodiversity.

This is evident in the Gulf Stream where the seasonal warmth of the sea is an important factor in maintaining both quantity and diversity. A few fishing companies have been experimenting with monitoring chlorophyll levels of the Gulf Stream to identify areas which are likely to attract fish due to the increase in plankton generated by the increased chlorophyll levels. This makes the fishing companies more efficient and reduces their environmental impact by reducing the amount of travel. In addition, scientists have been working on identifying the swimming channels of whales in the Atlantic to ensure that ships do not cross the channels and interfere with the whales' communication. These scientists have discovered that disruption to the whales' communication channels from the noise of ships has a negative effect on their breeding patterns. Every innovation in this area is useful for protecting the diversity of the oceans in the future. With scientists, conservationists and fishermen all working towards solutions, some progress is being made in man's relationship with the oceans' inhabitants.

QUESTIONS 1–5

*Complete the sentences with words from the passage. Use **NO MORE THAN THREE WORDS** for each answer.*

1 Pollution and excess fishing have caused a decrease in amounts of _____ marine diversity and stocks in the world's seas.

2 The use of _____ has caused a reduction in the quantity of small fish removed from the sea by the fishing industry.

3 Ocean temperature is _____ in making sure that the sea continues to have both variety and sufficient stocks of marine life.

4 According to experts, the _____ is damaging to the reproduction habits of whales in the Atlantic Ocean.

5 In order to safeguard the oceans of the future and the variety of marine life that inhabits them, each creative idea _____ .

8 Food

Countable nouns:

Objects, ideas and people that can be counted are called countable nouns. We can use articles and numbers with countable nouns. They can be singular or plural.

Approximately <u>2000 calories</u> per day are necessary for women to give them enough energy.	If you want specialist advice on food, the person you should see is <u>a nutritionist.</u>

Uncountable nouns:

Abstract ideas, qualities and materials that cannot be counted are called uncountable nouns. We cannot use the indefinite article or numbers with uncountable nouns. They are usually singular.

<u>Rice</u> is the main ingredient of many traditional Asian dishes.	The doctor advised against eating <u>food</u> such as <u>cheese</u>, which is high in <u>fat</u>.

Exceptions:

There are exceptions to the rules above.

1 Making uncountable nouns countable. By using a countable quantifying expression we can change a noun from uncountable to countable: *tea – a pot of tea*, *advice – a bit of advice*, *rice – a bowl of rice*, *coffee – a cup of coffee*

She ordered two <u>cups of coffee</u>.

2 When a noun has two meanings. Some nouns have an uncountable and a countable meaning.
  1. *glass* (material) + 2. *a glass of water* (liquid), 1. *business* (general) + 2. *a business* (company)

The restaurant walls are made entirely of <u>glass</u>.	Could I have <u>a glass of water</u> please?

3 Plural uncountable nouns. Some uncountable nouns only have a plural form and take a plural verb, e.g. *goods*, *clothes*, *trousers*, *stairs*

My <u>trousers were</u> completely ruined after I sat on the chewing gum.

Quantifiers:

Quantifiers are used with countable and uncountable nouns as follows:

	Countable	Uncountable
some	Some top chefs in the world are men.	Everyone needs to eat some protein every day.
any	Have we got any tomatoes?	There isn't any salad left in the fridge.
many/a lot of	Many children do not eat enough vegetables.	-
much/a lot of	-	We don't eat much meat these days.
few	There are few nutritional benefits in fast food.	-
a few	Eating a few nuts every day provides vitamin B.	-
little	-	Teenagers have little interest in cooking.
a little	-	A little milk is good for digestion.

Note: Much is used in negative sentences and questions. *Much* can be used in positive sentences when there is a modifying adverb (such as *too*, *so* or *as*) and with some abstract nouns.

Practice exercises

> **Grammar Tip:** Remember that *a few* and *a little* are used in a positive way, for example:
>
> *There are a few reasons for eating complex fats.* (there are some reasons)
>
> *We have a little evidence for consuming more fat in our diet.* (there is some evidence)
>
> However, *few* and *little* are used in a negative way, for example:
>
> *There are few reasons for eating complex fats.* (there are almost no reasons)
>
> *We have little evidence for consuming more fat in our diet.* (there is almost no evidence)

1 **Complete the sentences 1–8 using the words in the box.**

a bowl of soup	much	soup	meat	some	few	meats

1 Vegetarianism is the practice of not eating _____ for either ethical or health reasons.

2 Many people think that there are _____ advantages to taking vitamin pills as vitamins are found in most fruit and vegetables.

3 The company makes _____ using only organic ingredients.

4 Many _____ can be part of the British traditional roast dinner, including beef, pork or chicken.

5 In the winter I usually heat _____ and have _____ bread with it for my lunch.

6 I don't drink _____ water. I suppose I should drink more.

2 Listen to a student conducting a survey on eating habits and complete the notes below using NO MORE THAN THREE WORDS AND/OR A NUMBER.

Student 1: eating habits

Name: ..... Jim ......

Degree course: ..... Biology ......

Eating habits: ..... Doesn't eat (1) _meat_ ~~meat~~ because it's too expensive.

Regularly has vegetable-based (2) _meal_ for lunch and dinner.

Thinks his diet is too high in (3) ~~non~~ - vegetarian meal .

Needs to replace with (4) _juice_ – currently only drinks (5) a couple of glasses daily.

3 There are seven errors in the answer below. Listen and correct the errors in the text.

> *Describe a nice meal that you remember. You should say:*
> - *What you ate*
> - *Where you went*
> - *What the occasion was*
>
> *And say why you liked it.*

Last year I went to a wonderful restaurant overlooking the river in my city, Marseille, with a group of friends. The special occasion was my friend's 21st birthday and we decided to go out for dinner. We wanted to eat a beef because this restaurant is famous for meat, but as we arrived late they didn't have many beefs left. Instead we ate bouillabaisse which is a kind of seafood stew containing a fish and shellfish. I had a couple of glasses of orange juice. For dessert we each had a slice of birthday cakes which the restaurant had made especially for my friend. The cake had 21 candle and my friend blew them all out in one go so she made much wishes for the future. We had so many fun that night.
much

> **Exam tip:** In the IELTS Speaking Part 2 you often need to be able to describe people, places, experiences and objects. Understanding the correct use of countable and uncountable nouns will help your fluency.

Exam practice: Speaking Part 2

Read the following prompt for an IELTS Speaking exam Part 2. Give yourself one minute to prepare and make notes. Then speak for one to two minutes on the topic.

Describe a traditional dish from your country. You should say:

- What it is made from
- How to cook it
- When people eat it

And say why you like or dislike it.

12

Now listen to the model answer.

Make some notes on how you could improve your answer based on the model answer.

E.g. *I didn't have all the vocabulary for cooking that I needed – look it up and learn more vocabulary for key topics!*

_____

_____

_____

_____

_____

_____

9 Employment and finance

The definite article (the): *The* is used mainly with singular nouns:

1   When the listener/reader knows which noun we are talking about, either because it has been mentioned before or it is clear which one:

There is a new employment law on retirement ages. In my opinion, <u>the</u> law is unfair.	I think <u>the</u> government needs to renew its economic policy.

2   When the speaker/writer qualifies a noun with information to make it definite:

You know, <u>the</u> minister who was sacked because he was taking bribes.

3   Where there is only one of something:

<u>The</u> world is suffering from this economic downturn.

4   With '*the ... of ...*' and '*the ... of a ...*' (for definite noun phrases)

<u>The</u> rate of inflation is rising.	I noticed <u>the</u> papers of a fellow commuter on the train.

5   With superlatives, with geographical features and weather, and with well-defined groups:

He is <u>the</u> hardest working employee in the company.	I couldn't get to work because of <u>the</u> fog.	<u>The</u> bankers have put this country into a state of crisis.

The indefinite article (a/an): *A/an* is used with singular nouns:

1   When the listener/reader does not know the thing we are referring to because it is mentioned for the first time or is unspecific/unimportant:

There is <u>a</u> new employment law on retirement ages.	We need <u>an</u> assistant.

2   When using adjectives before a noun:

High taxation on the rich is <u>a</u> very unfair system.

3   When using quantities such as fractions and large numbers to mean 'one':

<u>a</u> third, <u>a</u> million, <u>a</u> hundred

4   When we talk about one member of a group or class:

<u>An</u> employer must be aware of employment law. (any employer)	He's <u>a</u> banker. (one of a job type)

No article is used:

1 When referring to a noun in general (this is common in academic writing). Usually the noun is in the plural:

<u>Jobs</u> are essential if you want to make money.	<u>Economics</u> is an essential part of <u>politics</u>.

2 With uncountable nouns, when the noun is not a specific group:

Jobs are essential if you want to make <u>money</u>.

3 With most proper nouns (names):

She works for <u>Google</u>.	I have another bank account in <u>Switzerland</u>.

Note: These rules cover most article usage, but as so often in grammar, there are exceptions.

Practice exercises

1   **Complete the spaces with *the*, *a*, *an* or no article (–) and write the rule numbers.**

   1   Economic advisors to _____ government warned against not regulating larger businesses.
         Rule: _____

   2   I believe that there should be _____ system to manage economic instability.
         Rule: _____

   3   _____ inflation is a constant worry for _____ employers.   *Rule:* _____ *Rule:* _____

   4   _____ Toyota has one of _____ highest revenues for any company in Japan.
         Rule: _____ *Rule:* _____

   5   Every company needs _____ good staff.   *Rule:* _____

   6   My father is _____ employment lawyer.   *Rule:* _____

   7   _____ world economy, although presently unstable, will soon recover.   *Rule:* _____

   > **Grammar tip:** Proper nouns or names, can sometimes take articles. The best way to decide is to think of whether the proper noun is a part of a group. If it is, then it may take *the*, e.g. *the UN* (a group of nations), *the United States* (a group of states), *the Seychelles* (a group of islands).

2   **Complete the spaces in the text below with *the*, *a*, *an* or no article (–).**

   (1) _a_ third of all employees in (2) _the_ UK see 'taking a sickie' as an acceptable part of (3) _–_ work, nothing more than light-hearted flexibility with working hours, yet taking days off when not actually sick is costing (4) _the_ economy (5) _–_ billions of pounds (6) _a_ year in (7) _the_ UK alone. As such, (8) _the_ reasons for these days off of work need to be addressed to counteract (9) _the_ 'sick culture' embracing society.

   The reasons for these 'sick' days are quite complex. One of (10) _the_ main reasons for this kind of absence is 'work fatigue', (11) _the_ fact that (12) _–_ people are bored with their jobs. As one leading professor states, 'jobs have become more fragmented and as such, people cannot give meaning to their work and feel alienated from their main roles. This can be seen by (13) _the_ masses of people who are sitting at (14) _a_ workstation every day for seven or eight hours doing a job which is only one small part of a process.' Bringing back this kind of meaning into work could be (15) _a_ difficult task, one which may not even be possible.

However, (16) _the_ most cited reason for taking 'sick days' is (17) _✓_ family commitments, such as childcare or illness within (18) _the_ family. This is an issue which can be addressed with such things as (19) _✓_ flexible working hours and home working. Perhaps, if employers can be a bit more forward thinking in these areas, they will, in the long run, be (20) _the_ ones to benefit the most.

> **Exam tip:** Articles can give you a clue to answers in sentence completion/summary completion questions.

3   Complete the sentences using words from the text in exercise 2.

1   Billions of pounds are lost through unjustified 'sick' days, and _____ for this need to be looked at.

2   As much as a _____ of workers see these sick days as acceptable.

3   Work fatigue is when _____ with their work.

4   Changing people's perspectives of their jobs might be a _____.

5   Problems within _____ are the most common reason for this kind of leave-taking.

4   Find and correct the mistakes in the following Part 1 Writing sample. There are eight mistakes in the use of articles.

Millionaires in the USA, by main profession

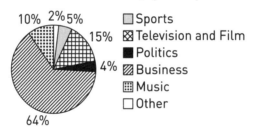

10% 2% 5%   ☐ Sports
          15% ☒ Television and Film
          ■ Politics
          4%   ▨ Business
               ▦ Music
               ☐ Other
64%

The pie chart shows the main careers of millionaires in the United States in percentages. We can see that a majority of millionaires are businesspeople, while other jobs such as in the entertainment or the politics only represent small proportion of the total. However, it could be said that millionaires are mostly people in the business and entertainment industries.

In the USA, people who work in a business account for just under two thirds of millionaires. Next largest group of millionaires on the chart is people who work in film and television. They account for 15% of the total. This group is closely followed by people who work in music. This sector accounts for the tenth of all millionaires in the USA.

The smaller groups all make up fewer than ten per cent of millionaires when combined. These people are sportspeople, politicians and people in other careers. The smallest group is an 'other' group with two per cent.

Exam practice: Writing Task 1

You should spend about 20 minutes on this task.

The graph below shows the percentage of part-time workers in each country of the United Kingdom in 1980 and 2010.

Summarize the information by selecting and reporting the main features, and make comparisons where relevant.

Write at least 150 words.

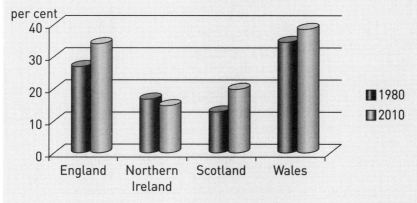

The percentage of part-time workers in each country of the United Kingdom

Exam tip: In Writing Task 1, it is essential to understand what the graph or chart is representing. Look closely at the information in the instructions as well as all details of the graph or chart.

The graph in this task shows the percentage of part-time workers in **each country** of the UK. The following are **incorrect** statements:

- *Wales had more part-time workers than England.* (The graph is in percentages, not numbers)
- *England had 25% of part-time workers in 1980.* (The countries do not add up to 100% so England did not have 25% of all part-time workers. The graph shows that 25% of the <u>population of England</u> worked part time.)

Now compare what you wrote with the model answer in the answer key.

10 Youth

Signposting: Signposting is seen in both speech and writing as a way to organize content and make it clear to the listener or reader where the content is going, for example by:

Ordering main points: Use: *firstly, secondly, next, finally, lastly*

Ordering a process or narrative: Use: *first, then, after that, afterwards*

Giving examples: Use: *for instance, for example*

Summarizing: Use: *in conclusion, in summary*

All of these signposting words can be followed by a comma and a clause.

> Firstly, there are many activities youths can become involved in.

In speech, many can be followed by a noun, verb or adjective.

> Today I am going to look at youth problems. Firstly, alienation. Then, peer pressure. And lastly, anti-social behaviour.

This cannot be done in writing.

Linking words and phrases: These words link ideas together so that speech or writing can be followed clearly.

Positioning of linking words: Linking words can be positioned in a variety of ways within a sentence. Here you can see a simplified guide to the main constructions:

1	*Link word* + Noun, Clause	OR	Clause + *Link word* + Noun
2	*Link word*, + Clause		
3	Clause 1, *Link word* + Clause 2		
4	*Link word* + Clause 1, + Clause 2		

Different linking words have different functions and need different constructions:

Addition: *in addition* (2), *in addition to* (1), *moreover* (2), *furthermore* (2), *and* (3)

Contrast: *however* (2), *in contrast* (2), *in contrast to* (1), *whereas* (3/4), *although* (3/4), *even though* (3/4), *yet* (3), *but* (3)

Reasons: *due to* (1), *because* (3/4), *because of* (1), *as* (3/4)

Results: *therefore* (2/3), *so* (1/3), *as a result* (2), *as a result of* (1)

Repetition: *in other words* (2), *by that I mean* (2)

> **Grammar Tip:** Using linking words and phrases correctly is essential. When learning a new linking word, use a good dictionary to look at how it should be used within and/or across sentences.

Practice exercises

1   Decide on the correct linking or signposting word and finish the sentences. Then write the function. **There may be more than one correct answer.**

*Example: I will look at the effects of peer pressure, **and** how young people can avoid peer pressure.*
*Function: **Addition***

1   There are not enough activities for teenagers in the area. _____, many teenagers just socialize in the streets in the evenings. *Function:* _____

2   _____ dealing with the results of youth crime, we must address the causes. *Function:* _____

3   Today I am going to talk about youth projects in the local area. Firstly, I will talk about the sports projects. Then, I will talk about the cultural projects. _____, I will talk about the volunteering opportunities. *Function:* _____

4   Many students cannot get a place at university _____ rising tuition fees. *Function:* _____

5   Teenagers are the future of this country, _____ many people ignore their needs. *Function:* _____

6   This talk has looked at many of the positive and negative aspects of vocational courses for teens. _____, although there are some drawbacks to these courses, overwhelmingly they are a good thing. *Function:* _____

2   Listen to the lecture and complete the gaps 1–6 in the notes using no more than three words in each space.
(Track 13)

Youth initiatives in the UK

1   (1) _____ schemes
      cheap and (2) _____

2   Sports clubs
      numerous but (3) _____

3   (4) _____ clubs
      lack of numbers ⎫
      expense   ⎬ = (5) Not _____
      accommodation problems ⎭
      In summary, (6)_____ need to be found

3   Below is the audio script for the second part of the lecture. Decide on appropriate linking words to complete the spaces. There may be more than one possibility for each gap. Then listen to Track 14 on the CD and check your answers.
(Track 14)

So, what other initiatives could the government focus on? Well, (1) _____ the success of the sports clubs, new 'open spaces' initiatives are being discussed, (2) _____ football tournaments in local playing fields or athletics days in local parks. This could regenerate local areas and renew interest in activities for young people. Staffing would still be necessary, (3) _____ young people could take an active role in organizing and managing competitions. This could cut down staff costs significantly.

(4) _____ the open spaces scheme, there has been discussion of reinvigorating the 'taste of work' scheme, which gives young people a chance to get work experience in a variety of jobs in their school holidays. (5) _____, this scheme has met with harsh criticism from some politicians who think that it is a way of providing a free workforce by stealth. In fact, I think it is fair to say that this scheme will not see any renewed interest (6) _____ these criticisms.

(7) _____, the scheme that there has been a lot of talk about is the outward bound activities courses, or OBAC for short. This has been successful in many other countries, (8) _____ Canada, Mexico and Brazil. The activity courses give young people a chance to get out into the countryside and enjoy nature. (9) _____ this, they also give teens a chance to learn life skills and experience adventure on a broader scale.

4   Read the following text and put the events 1–7 in the correct order.

> **The History of BUNAC**
>
> BUNAC, the organization which sends young people overseas to live and work, will be celebrating its 50th anniversary next year. It grew from North American Clubs at London Universities who wanted students from both countries to be able to live and work in the other country for a short time. This became a reality as a result of the introduction of the EVP (Exchange Visa Programme) and subsequently the SEEP (Student Employment Exchange Programme). Due to the massive rising popularity of the British-American scheme, programmes started running firstly in Canada and then in locations in the rest of the world.

1   The SEEP programme started
2   The scheme grew in popularity
3   British and American students wanted to travel more freely in each other's country
4   The EVP programme began
5   British and American students could travel more freely in each other's country
6   The scheme started in Canada
7   The scheme started in other countries

Exam practice: Reading – completing a table

Complete the table opposite with words from the following text. Use NO MORE THAN THREE WORDS for each answer.

The Life and Death of Punk

Although the punk movement didn't gain cultural popularity until the late 1970's, the origins of the subculture stemmed from the cultural scenes in the UK and USA earlier in the decade with.

radical musicians such as The Velvet Underground and new thinkers like Malcolm McClaren. As with any subculture, the first stage must be the birth of the subculture which is led by cultural leaders. These leaders inspire the styles and values that will become part of the subculture. In the case of punk, McClaren was very much the stylist of the punk look, selling daring clothes that the punk culture came to embrace.

Punk began in its fullest form in the 1970s, when the daring and anti-establishment concepts of these pioneers took a more popular form. Punk sprang up largely as a result of a weakening economy and high levels of unemployment. Social and political problems are often the reason behind the next stage of subcultural development; the subcultural embrace. This is when the subculture is at its most dynamic, and is becoming increasingly accepted.

After that the subculture plateaus. This is when it becomes stable and people demonstrate sub-norms which include shared ways of dressing, shared values and beliefs, and shared forms of film or music. In terms of punks, this can be seen in such things as Mohawks, a particularly striking hairstyle, and piercings. Punks often have many facial piercings which make them stand out from the norm. This need for individualism is quite strong in youth subcultures, yet at the same time is a contradiction because these very people are copying from within their groups. A striking feature at this stage is the onset of deviant subcultures, which take some characteristics of the main subculture and distort these with other characteristics. As well as often exhibiting anti-social behaviour, they distance themselves from the main subculture by mutual dislike. In the culture of punk, skinheads are an apt example of this, exhibiting all the key features of a deviant subculture.

The important thing to note now is that whereas the main subculture continues through the cultural plateau to then suffer from eventual rejection, the deviant subculture continues for much longer. A youth subculture usually fades away after an amount of time as it becomes more and more old-fashioned; something which young people never like to be associated with. The 'accepted' subcultures are then replaced by a newer and more cutting-edge subculture, in the case of punk, dance and new romantic subcultures emerged which saw the end of the established subculture of punk.

The Life Span of a Youth Subculture

Stage	Description	Relation to punk movement
1. subculture 1 _____	Styles and values of subcultures initiated by cultural pioneers	e.g. pioneers like Malcolm McClaren
2. subcultural 2 _____	Often a reaction to socio-political issues	e.g. economic decline and 3 _____
3. subcultural plateau	Identified in development of shared behavioural, attitudinal, fashion, and musical 4 _____	e.g. Mohawks, piercings
creation of a deviant subculture	Often characterized by 5 _____ and main subculture rejection	e.g. skinheads
4. 6 _____	Caused by ageing of the subculture	e.g. rise of dance and new romantics

11 People and places

Structures that show unequal comparisons:

1 *more/less* + adjective/adverb + *than*

Living in the countryside is <u>healthier than</u> living in a city.	Traffic in towns moves <u>more slowly than</u> in villages.

2 *more/fewer/less* + noun/noun phrase + *than*

There are <u>more people</u> in this town <u>than</u> there used to be.	There are <u>fewer supermarkets</u> in country villages <u>than</u> in regional towns.

3 *not as* + adjective/adverb + *as*

This town is <u>not as prosperous as</u> the others in this region.	The people in London <u>aren't as friendly as</u> those in my home town.

4 *not as* + *much/many* + noun/noun phrase + *as*

<u>Not as many people visit New Zealand as Australia</u>.	There <u>isn't as much sun in the north of the country as in the south</u>.

Structures that show equal comparisons:

1 *as* + adjective/adverb + *as*

The office buildings in Paris are <u>as beautiful as</u> the monuments.	Contrary to popular belief life in a large village moves <u>as quickly as</u> in a town.

2 *as* + *much/many* + noun/noun phrase + *as*

There <u>are as many immigrants as</u> tourists in London.	You can visit <u>as many historic castles in Scotland as</u> in Wales

3 *the same* + noun/noun phrase + *as*

In every country you can find <u>the same type of people as</u> in your own.	I am interested in <u>the same lifestyle as</u> my parents.

Making comparisons stronger:

Add *much*, *far*, *a lot*, *considerably* or *not nearly* before *more/less* or before an adjective/adverb

Inter-city travel is <u>far faster</u> than it was ten years ago.	There are <u>considerably more</u> people moving abroad from the UK to Spain <u>than</u> France.

Making comparisons weaker:

Add *a bit*, *a little*, *nearly*, *almost*, *not much* or *not a lot* before *as* or an adjective/adverb

It's <u>nearly</u> as easy to travel by train as by car.	Walking briskly is actually <u>a little quicker</u> than using public transport in the city centre.

> See page 119 in the Grammar reference for more information.

Practice exercises

1   Decide if the following pairs of sentences have the same meaning or a different meaning. Write S (same) or D (different).

   1   The Coliseum is not nearly as old as Stonehenge.

   Stonehenge is considerably younger than The Coliseum.   _____

   2   In Europe the same percentage of people live in flats as live in houses.

   As many people live in houses as live in flats in Europe.   _____

   3   This village isn't nearly as picturesque as the last one we visited.

   This village is almost as picturesque as the last one we visited.   _____

   4   Urbanization in Asia has been increasing more quickly than in Europe.

   In Asia, urbanization hasn't been increasing as quickly as in Europe.   _____

   5   Our new house in the suburbs has got as much space as our old house in the city centre.

   Our new house in the suburbs is as spacious as our old house in the
   city centre.   _____

   6   You can walk between places in the city centre as easily as taking public transport.

   You can walk between places in the city centre more easily than taking
   public transport.   _____

2   Read the examiner questions from a Speaking Part 1 conversation and expand the answer notes into full sentences. Try to use comparative structures where possible. The first one has been done as an example.

   1   **Examiner:** *How has the place you live in changed recently?*

   Notes: more traffic nowadays, lots of people have moved here for work, the city is richer now

Example: Well, in my city there is a lot more traffic than there used to be. This is because of the new business centre, which has brought a lot more people to the city for work. This has made the city richer than it was. In fact that's the most significant difference – the city is not as poor as it was 10 years ago.

2 Examiner: *So, you're studying here in Sydney. How is your town/city different from Sydney?*

Notes: different shop opening hours, more efficient transport system, same weather

_____

_____

_____

3 Examiner: *Is it a good place to live?*

Notes: better than other cities in my country, more modern, lots of parks, not crowded like other cities

_____

_____

_____

Now listen and read the audio script for Task 15. Compare your answers to the suggested answers.

> **Exam tip:** Comparative structures can be tested in the IELTS Listening exam by changing positive and negative structures. For example, in the exam you might hear: *In this town there are far more visitors to the church than the town hall.* and the question or correct answer might be: *Not nearly as many people visit the town hall as the church in this town.*

3 **Listen to three students discussing a presentation they have to give for their social studies class. Choose the correct answer A, B or C to complete sentences 1–3 below.**

1 James thinks that the topic of the presentation should be about

   A why families want to live in the countryside less than in the past

   B the reasons families are moving to the city more nowadays

   C how recently countryside living has become more desirable

2 Professor Davies told the students that

   A there are the same number of houses available in suburban areas as 20 years ago

   B more families have moved to cities over the last two decades

   C the range of options for families is less wide nowadays

3 Suzanne agrees with Helen because she thinks that the students should show that

   A they have researched more widely than the reading list

   B they have done more research than for their last presentation

   C they have done more research than necessary

> **Grammar tip:** To switch between positive and negative comparisons you can change the comparative structure: **a** the verb, **b** the nouns or **c** the adjective, for example:
>
> **a** *A city is noisier than a village. = A village isn't as noisy as a city.*
>
> **b** *Villages are less interesting than towns. = Towns are more interesting than villages.*
>
> **c** *A block of flats is taller than a house. = A house is smaller than a block of flats.*

4 Now rewrite the following sentences from the student conversation changing positive sentences to negative and negative to positive. More than one correct answer may be possible.

  1 The countryside has become more attractive to families nowadays.

  2 You've thought about the presentation a lot more clearly than me.

  3 We have done as much research for the presentation as we could.

  4 Our final grade won't be nearly as high as our last presentation.

Exam practice: Listening – multiple choice

> **Exam tip:** Make sure you check that the answer you choose matches the **meaning** of what you hear not just the **words** you hear.

QUESTIONS 1–4

Answer the questions below. Choose the correct letter A, B or C.

1 According to Kirsty, the students should

  A approach their project from the perspective suggested by Dr. Jones.

  B make the project less general than Dr. Jones suggested.

  C expand the project and make it more general.

2 How scientific was the voting system for the New Seven Wonders of the World?

  A It was more scientific than a talent show because people voted multiple times .

  B Due to the multiple voting system it was not as scientific as voting on the Internet.

  C It was much less scientific than the voting systems which are used in politics.

3 What do the students want to show in their project?

  A why some countries rely more heavily on tourism

  B that the type of people who vote affects the voting outcome

  C the advantages of the competition to find the New Seven Wonders of the World

4 Why does Greg think the project will be good?

  A Because the students will have done a lot of reading.

  B Because Dr. Jones is expecting the students to produce a better project than the last one.

  C Because the project will be different from those of their classmates.

12 Crime

Modal verbs can be used for present and future obligation and ability in the following ways:

Can is used:

1 to express ability

I <u>can</u> drive a car.

2 to request and give permission

<u>Can</u> I use your car? Yes, you <u>can</u>.

3 to say that something is allowed

You <u>can</u> eat in this room. (it is allowed)

Cannot (Can't) is used:

1 to express inability

I <u>can't</u> find my keys.

2 to deny permission

Can I use your car? No, you <u>can't</u>.

3 to say that something is not allowed

You <u>can't</u> take money! (it is not allowed)

Might/ May/Could is used:

1 to express possibility in the present/future

Prisons <u>might</u> become overcrowded. (it is possible)

2 In the negative; it is more common to use *mightn't/may not* in order to express negative possibility.

Should is used:

1 to express a recommendation

People <u>should</u> try to be kind to others. (it is a good thing to do)

2 in the negative to express a negative recommendation

> People shouldn't be horrible to others. (it is a bad thing to do)

Must is used:

from the speaker's point of view to express a strong obligation

> He must go to prison! (**I think** it is necessary)

Must not (Mustn't) is used:

from the speaker's point of view to say that something is not allowed

> You mustn't take money! (**I think** it is not allowed)

All of these modal verbs are used with another main verb and without *to*. There is no third person construction, e.g. *He **must go** to prison.* NOT *He ~~must to go~~ to prison.* OR *He **musts go** to prison.*

Modal constructions using 'to' (semi-modal verbs)

Ought to is used:

to express a recommendation (like *should*)

> *People **ought to** be kind to others.*

This construction is less common in the negative.

Have to is used:

to express a strong objective obligation

> People have to follow the law. (it is required)

Don't have to is used:

to express that something is a matter of choice and not necessary

> You don't have to pay the fine today. (you can pay today if you want, but it is not necessary)

Practice exercises

1 **Decide on the correct modal or semi-modal form and finish the sentences. There may be more than one answer.**

  1 I believe it is better for criminals to go to prison than to do community work.

  Criminals _____ to prison instead of doing community work.

  2 It is necessary to follow all the laws in a country.

  You _____ all the laws in a country.

3 I think it is possible that the crime rate will increase in future.

I think the crime rate _____ in future.

4 Sometimes offenders can choose between paying a fine or doing community service.

Sometimes offenders _____. They can do community service instead.

5 Police officers are able to take early retirement because of the demands of their job.

Police officers _____ early retirement because of the demands of their job.

> **Grammar tip:** Always use modal verbs to express possibility and likelihood. Only use *will* when the information is factual and not your opinion, for example:
>
> The crime rate **might** decrease as a result of the new laws. (you cannot be sure)
> The government **will** introduce new laws next month to help reduce crime. (this is a fact)

2 Sentences 1–5 are from an IELTS Writing Task 2 essay. The student has used verbs that are too strong (e.g. *will*) or incorrect. Decide on the correct modal form. There may be more than one answer.

1 Criminals who don't have a strong enough punishment <u>will</u> reoffend. _____

2 People <u>won't</u> pay attention to the law if it is not strict enough. _____

3 Euthanasia <u>must</u> be legalized in all countries. _____

4 People who commit crime <u>must</u> go to prison so they can learn good behaviour.

_____

🎧 **3** Below is a response to an IELTS Speaking Part 3 question. There are mistakes in some of the sentences, both in terms of modal choice and construction. Correct the mistakes, then listen to the recording and check your answers. There are six mistakes.

18

Examiner: How can crime be prevented?
Student: Crime prevention musts start from education. If people are not raised well, then they will commit crimes in the future. It's the responsibility of both parents and schools to educate children in the difference between right and wrong. This could be done in special ethics classes in schools, and perhaps parenting classes mightn't be a good idea for parents who are unsure of how to raise children with more moral values. These classes shouldn't be compulsory though as this might to be too expensive and unnecessary. However, although all parents mustn't go, it could be useful for those who are struggling. More information will help these parents.

4 In Part 3 of the Speaking exam, you need to talk about your ideas. You can often do this using modal verbs to give recommendations.

Look at the following questions and answers. How could you continue the answers using modals? The first one is done for you.

Examiner: *Do you think crime is increasing nowadays?*
Student: *I don't think so. I think we just see more about crime on the TV and in newspapers. I think we shouldn't be too worried about crime, otherwise people might be scared to do the things they normally do in case something happens.*

Examiner: What are the best ways to prevent crimes?
Student: I think a certain amount of crime could be prevented with education. _____

_____

_____

_____

Examiner: Are any crimes acceptable?
Student: Yes, I think some crimes are more acceptable than others. For example we can't compare murder and driving too fast.

_____

_____

_____

Examiner: Are there any crimes which you think shouldn't be crimes?
Student: Yes, I think some small crimes, shouldn't be crimes.

_____

_____

_____

Exam practice: Speaking Part 3

You will hear five questions. Answer them as fully as possible. In this exam practice, you will have 30 seconds between questions to give your answers.

> **Speaking exam tip:** In Speaking Part 3 you should try to develop your answers as much as possible. Answer the question directly in your first sentence and then move on to do one or more of the following:
> – Give reasons for your answer
> – Add more information / develop your answer
> – Give examples of what you mean

Now listen to the model answers given by the student on Track 20 of the CD. How were they better than or different from your answers?

13 The planet

Past modal verbs differ greatly in use from the present modal verbs, even though they look similar.

Modal verbs for deduction in the past:

Must/mustn't is used *from the speaker's point of view to express a strong likelihood in the past*
must/mustn't + have + past participle   OR   must/mustn't + have + been + past participle

> The prime minister <u>mustn't have kept</u> his promise about increasing alternative energy forms, as I've seen nothing in the news about it. (**I think** it was likely he didn't keep his promise)

Note: Mustn't can be replaced by couldn't for the same meaning.

Might/may/could is used *to express possibility in the past*
might/may/could + have + past participle (Also might/may/could + have + been + verb(-ing))

> A curb on the use of fossil fuels <u>might have curtailed</u> the pollution problem. (it was possible)

Note: Modal verbs of deduction (must/could/might/may +be) can also be used in the present, but it is unlikely that you will see this in an IELTS exam.

Modal verbs for past ability:

Could is used:

1 *To express ability*

> I <u>could</u> swim 100 metres, but I can't now.

2 *To say that something was allowed*

> People <u>could travel</u> without a passport 200 years ago. (it was allowed)

Could not (couldn't) is used:

1 *To express inability*

> I <u>couldn't</u> complete my essay on global warming.

2 *To say that something was not allowed*

> He <u>couldn't</u> go into the monkey enclosure. (it was not allowed)

Had to is used *to express a strong objective obligation in the past*

People <u>had to travel</u> to Australia on a ship before air travel was invented. (it was necessary)

Didn't have to is used *to express that something was not an obligation*

I <u>didn't have to go</u> to work when I was a child.

Note: *Must* cannot be used in the past to express an obligation or choice.

Modal Verbs used for past regrets:

Should is used *to express a recommendation or regret in the past*
should + *have* + past participle (Also *should* + *have* + *been* + verb(-*ing*))

We <u>should have gone</u> on that Eco tourism trip. I'm sorry that we didn't. (we didn't go and I regret it)
We <u>shouldn't have gone</u> on that Eco tourism trip. It was expensive and dull. (we went and I regret it)

Ought to is also used *to express a recommendation or regret in the past*
ought to + *have* + past participle (Also *ought to* + *have* + *been* + verb(-*ing*))

We <u>ought to have</u> thought more about the planet before using so much fuel.

This construction is less common in the negative.

Practice exercises

1   **Decide on an appropriate past modal verb and the correct form of the verb in brackets to finish the sentences. There may be more than one correct answer.**

   1   When fossil fuels were discovered, people _____ (*know*) the negative effects they would eventually cause as no research had been done on them.

   2   In early civilisations, people _____ (*hunt*) for their own meat.

   3   People _____ (*take*) more care of endangered species. Over a hundred species have become extinct in the last 50 years and it's a terrible shame.

   4   It _____ (*be*) difficult to survive in the days before modern medicine and hygiene standards.

   5   A new lizard has been discovered in the rainforests of Sumatra. Some experts say they _____ (*inhabit*) the deeper rainforests for up to a million years.

   6   People _____ (*travel*) across borders quite easily in the past. Nowadays there are many more immigration rules.

   7   Before organised forms of rule such as kingdoms or governments, people _____ (*pay*) taxes.

   8   Resentment among the citizens _____ (*develop*) for a long time before the overthrow of the Empire, because popular support for a revolt had been growing for decades.

2   Complete the spaces in the following text using the options in the box.

didn't have to	shouldn't have	could
might have	had to	couldn't have

LIFE DURING THE ICE AGE

During the Ice Age in Europe, approximately 15,000 years ago, the winter weather was bleak. However, modern humans found ingenious methods for managing this extreme cold. In fact, these humans (1) _____ been the first to develop a range of skills and technological advances that are still with us today! Due to the freezing temperatures, these humans (2) _____ create things that could protect them from the environment. Early Europeans used the skin and bones from wild animals to make clothing and shelter.

Thankfully, they (3) _____ worry so much about their food. They (4) _____ kill their food effectively as they had developed sophisticated tools. When food was abundant, they buried supplies in the permafrost; an ancient form of deep-freezing. The unfortunate thing about their hunting and survival skills was that they slaughtered many of the animals to extinction. All we now have to remember them by is the cave paintings. Perhaps it could be argued that they (5) _____ killed these animals, but we cannot say what we would have done in the same situation.

Although life (6) _____ been easy for these people, they managed to survive and introduce art, language and behaviours that characterize people today; we owe a lot to their developments.

3   Decide on the correct past modal verb and complete the gaps in the conversation. Then listen and check your answers.

21

Kelly: Hi everyone. So, let's get started on our essay. Mark, have you done the research from last week?

Mark: Well, yes and no. I was trying to follow up on the suggestions from the lecture and I searched the library for books and journals. But I (1) _____ find anything relevant to our topic.

Louise: Well, maybe you were too late. We got the essay title two weeks ago so other students (2) _____ taken out all the books already.

Mark: Yes, I guess so.

Kelly: It doesn't sound likely to me. All the books (3) _____ been taken out – there's lots of books about astronomy in the main library.

Mark: Well, there was one book but I (4) _____ borrow it because it's a reference only book.

Kelly: Mm. We (5) _____ started this project earlier. What are we going to do now?

Louise: The other students (6) _____ been very keen to start! Well, don't worry. Why don't we just reserve the books we want? I've found some articles we can start reading now and then we'll be more focused for when the other students return the books we need.

22

3 **Listen to three students preparing a presentation and complete the notes below:**

Expedition details

Problem: Originally setting the camp up at the (1) _____ because of the (2) _____ season.

Solution: Setting the camp up at the (3) _____.

Discoveries:

New (4) _____ at the bottom of the mountain.
Halfway up the mountain (5) _____ were found and identified correctly due to
(6) _____ equipment.

Timescale: Arrived at the top of the mountain within (7) _____.

Exam practice: Listening – completing a table

> **Exam tip:** When completing a table, look at the headings in the table to try to predict what information you are looking for. The numbers on the answer spaces will tell you what order the information will be presented in.

23

Listen to three students talking about their essays and complete the table. **WRITE NO MORE THAN THREE WORDS AND/OR A NUMBER** for each answer:

	Andrew	Penny	Terry
TOPIC	Interesting subject choice	Should have made it more **1** _____	Agrees with **2** _____
WORK FOCUS ISSUES	Difficult to find **3** _____ on statistics	Concentrated on plate movement	Not **4** _____ on future predictions
RESEARCH FINDINGS	Earthquakes could have been predicted	The Earth is **5** _____	Needs to refocus

14 Globalization

Conditional structures are used to talk about conditions and results. The condition is something that must happen first in order for something else to happen as a result or consequence.

> **Grammar tip:** Conditional structures are usually presented as types (zero, first, second, third, mixed) using specific structures. It is important to remember that these specific structures are a general guide and that different tenses can be used in the condition clause. There are also alternatives to *will/would* in the result clause.

Zero conditional is used to talk about factual or true information. We can use *if* or *when* to introduce the condition.

Nowadays <u>when</u> we <u>communicate</u> across cultures, we usually <u>use</u> English.

First conditional is used to talk about future situations based on conditions.

<u>If</u> the world <u>continues</u> to focus on international trade, we <u>will need</u> to make our education systems more global.

Second conditional is used to speculate on something that we think is impossible.

<u>If</u> we <u>didn't have</u> cheap transport, we <u>wouldn't have</u> global products.

Third conditional is used to speculate about past events. It is often used to express regret or to imagine a different result of a past situation.

People <u>would have exchanged</u> ideas much earlier <u>if</u> the government <u>had changed</u> the laws on information protection during the 1990s.

Mixed conditional is used to express the present result of a past situation or explain how a present situation affected a past action. To do this we use a combination of second and third conditionals.

Transnational corporations <u>wouldn't exist</u> <u>if</u> globalization <u>hadn't become</u> the dominant form of trade in modern society.	<u>If</u> capitalism <u>wasn't</u> so popular, globalization <u>may not have happened</u> so quickly.

Other conditional structures/forms: There are other words and phrases which have a similar meaning to *if* and are used to express conditions. Some of these are *suppose/supposing (that)*, *provided/providing (that)*, *on condition (that)*, *as/so long as*, *unless* (meaning *if not*).

<u>Providing</u> technological progress <u>continues</u> at its current speed, we<u>'ll be interacting</u> with a much wider range of nationalities in the near future.	<u>Unless</u> we <u>control</u> globalization, national identity <u>will decline</u> sharply.

See page 120/1 in the Grammar reference for more information.

Practice exercises

1 Decide on the correct conditional form and finish the sentences using the verbs in brackets. Decide which conditional from page 58 matches the meaning of each sentence.

   1 The restaurant _____ (not go) out of business if that international burger company _____ (not open) last year. Conditional: _____

   2 When teenagers _____ (buy) technology, they usually _____ (want) the same products as all their friends. Conditional: _____

   3 As long as international travel _____ (continue), people _____ (stay) closely connected. Conditional: _____

   4 We _____ (not communicate) so successfully nowadays if technology _____ (developed) more slowly. Conditional: _____

   5 If more people _____ (be connected) via the Internet, communication _____ (be) easier. Conditional: _____

2 Complete the spaces in this student essay with conditional clauses. You can complete the spaces in any way using your own ideas. The first one has been done for you.

> **Exam tip:** Conditional structures can be useful for the IELTS Writing Task 2 to express facts or unreal situations based on conditions or to speculate on results or consequences in the future or past.

"Globalization is creating a world of one culture and destroying national identity."

To what extent do you agree with this statement?

Globalization has had a considerable effect on the world in the last few decades. While some people believe that these effects are all positive it can also be argued that globalization is destroying the identity of many countries in the world. This is because aspects of our lives such as entertainment, communication, products and business are similar in many parts of the world. This essay will argue that globalization is destroying national identity for three reasons.

Firstly, in terms of entertainment young people are less interested in their local culture and this could have dangerous consequences. If young people do not know about their cultural heritage (1) they will not understand the older generation. As a result, there could be serious communication breakdowns within cultures.

In addition, globalization has produced large corporations which often prevent local businesses from making money. Many people only want to buy branded products from these international companies. Unless governments do something to limit the influence of these companies, (2) _____

Finally, there is the problem of language. Due to globalization English has become the most important language in the world and many languages are beginning to die out. This is a negative aspect of globalization and could have serious consequences in the future. If everyone has to speak English in the future and not their own native language (3) _____

In conclusion, globalization is having negative effects on national identity and people should focus more on their local culture. If we allow globalization to continue to dominate local cultures, in the future (4) _____

3 For the topic of globalization, predict some Speaking Part 3 questions. Two examples have been done for you.

1 How has globalization affected the way we communicate?

2 As a result of globalization, English has become the world language. Do you think this is a positive or negative result?

3 _____
_____
_____
_____

4 _____
_____
_____
_____

5 _____
_____
_____
_____

6 _____
_____
_____
_____

Now listen to the questions on Track 24 of the CD and note them down. Are any similar to your questions?

> **Exam tip:** For the Speaking exam it is a good idea to practise predicting questions for typical IELTS topics to help you think about how to use high level grammar in your answers. Using more complex structures such as conditionals will increase your chances of getting a higher band score.

4 Read the examiner questions below and think about how you could answer them using a conditional. Then answer the questions using conditional structures. Write down the type(s) of conditional you used in your answer. The first example has been done for you.

1 Examiner question: How do you think globalization might change the world in the future?

> **Student answer:** _I think that <u>if globalization continues</u> to develop, young people of the future <u>will have</u> a different understanding of things like nationality and culture._

Conditional: __First conditional__

2 **Examiner question:** Has globalization caused young people to care less about their countries?

Conditional: _____

3 **Examiner question:** What would you say to someone who thinks that globalization is ruining the world?

Conditional: _____

4 **Examiner question:** Can globalization make the world a more equal place?

Conditional: _____

25 Now listen to Track 25 on the CD and the model answers given by the student.

Exam practice: Speaking Part 3

Answer the questions on globalization below using the techniques from Unit 12 (giving reasons for your answer, adding more information, giving examples of what you mean). Try to use conditional structures where possible.

1 What are the main disadvantages of globalization?
2 Do you think globalization has made the world a better place?
3 How has globalization changed the way we travel and communicate?
4 How has globalization benefited people in your country?
5 What are the consequences of allowing large companies to sell their products all over the world?

26 Now listen to the model answers on Track 26 of the CD. How were they better or different to your answers?

_____

_____

_____

_____

_____

_____

15 Culture and modern society

Reported or indirect speech is used to report the words of another person. For example:

'I am an artist.' = She said that she was an artist.

In order to report another person's words we need to change the **tense**, **pronoun** and **time words** and use a **reporting verb** such as *say* or *tell*.

Say and tell:

Say and *tell* are the most common reporting verbs. *Say* never has an indirect object and uses a *that* clause. *Tell* always has an indirect object and uses a variety of structures.

He said that he was interested in philosophy.	He told me that he was interested in philosophy.

(see grammar reference for other *tell* structures)

Tense changes:

Some of the tenses of the original direct speech have to be changed in reported speech are as follows:

Present simple: 'I like opera.'	→ *past simple:* She said that she liked opera.
Past simple: 'We went to the theatre.'	→ *past perfect:* He said that they had gone to the theatre.
Past perfect: 'I had read the novel.'	→ *past perfect:* She said that she had read the novel.
Present modals (can, may, must, will): 'I'll start photography classes soon.'	→ *past modals (could, might, had to, would):* He said that he would start photography classes soon.

See page 122 in the Grammar reference for more information.

Reporting questions:

Wh- questions use a reporting verb such as *ask* or *enquire* + *wh-* question word (no auxiliary verb).

'When are you going to the gallery?'	She asked when I was going to the gallery

Yes/no questions use a reporting verb such as *ask* or *enquire* + *if/whether* (no auxiliary verb).

'Do you think children should be more creative?'	He asked me whether I thought children should be more creative.

Pronouns and time words: In reported speech pronouns and time words change.

| 'I'll give you my latest painting tomorrow.' | She said she would give me her latest painting the following day. |
| 'I went to an interesting exhibition yesterday.' | He told me that he had been to an interesting exhibition the previous day. |

Reporting verbs (advice, requests, orders, promises): There are many reporting verbs that express interpretation or judgment such as *advise, deny, recommend, argue, promise, warn, claim*. These verbs always have a specific structure that is necessary to learn.

| 'Don't see that film.' | She warned me not to see the film. | *to warn* + indirect object + *not* + infinitive |
| 'We think schools should teach more sociology' | They argued that schools should teach more sociology. | *to argue* + *that* + clause |

Note: In many reporting structures you can omit *that*.

> **Grammar tip:** Reporting verbs help you to understand the opinion of the speaker. Make sure you know the difference in meaning of common reporting verbs such as *argue, claim, deny, order, promise, recommend, suggest, warn*. For example, *argue* and *order* are much stronger than *claim* or *suggest*.

Practice exercises

1 **For questions 1–4 rewrite the sentences using reported speech. For questions 5–8 complete the sentence with the correct reporting verb structure. There may be more than one correct answer.**

1 'I went to the opera yesterday and really enjoyed it.' She said that _____

2 'The government has to invest more money in the arts.' He argued that _____

3 'This museum hasn't had any internationally recognized exhibitions for several years.' The critic announced that _____

4 'What does the theatre director intend to do to increase ticket sales?' The reporter asked _____

5 'If the cinema does not receive funding, it will have to close down.' The manager _____ if the cinema did not receive funding, it would have to close down.

6 'There has been a rapid rise in the number of people engaging in cultural activities over the last decade.' The politician _____ there had been a rapid rise in the number of people engaging in cultural activities over the previous decade.

7 'The decline in interest in art is not due to a lack of private investment in galleries.' The artist _____ the decline in interest in art was due to a lack of private investment in galleries.

8 'I think it would be a good idea to read *An Introduction to Sociology* to begin with.' The teacher _____ reading *An Introduction to Sociology* to begin with.

2   Answer the questions below using reported speech. Give yourself one minute to prepare, then talk for one or two minutes.

> *Describe a piece of advice that someone gave you. You should say:*
> * *Who gave you the advice*
> * *What the advice was*
> * *If you followed the advice and what happened*
>
> *And say if it was advice you would give to someone else.*

27   Now listen to the model answer on Track 27 of the CD and compare it with your answer. How many reporting verbs and reported speech structures did you use?

3   Read the text below and then complete the sentences with the correct verb forms.

The decline of poetry in the modern age

The decline of poetry readings as a form of mass entertainment in modern society has been well documented by academics and critics alike and there are various theories which may account for it. According to Professor Jackson at Barnes State University, the rise of various forms of popular culture such as music festivals, comedy and musical theatre means that it is not surprising that poetry is in decline. However, he also believes that 'the speed with which it has declined overall is surprising'. Professor Jackson has been criticized by Dr Arundell from Clivedale University who thinks that his research is misleading. 'Professor Jackson has misrepresented a change as a decline.' Dr Arundell's view is supported by the poet and writer, Sam Henderson, who states that 'people who attend poetry readings also frequent the cinema, musical theatre and classical concerts nowadays so the decline is not in the number of people but in the number of times these people attend poetry readings.' This subtle difference is the main conclusion of Dr Arundell's study. She would like poets and spoken word performers to use this information as the basis of widening their audience; as she argues, 'If poetry lovers have a wide range of cultural interests, then cinema or theatre goers will also have a wide range of interests.' She concludes that 'there is no reason why these people can't be urged to try poetry readings too.'

1   Professor Jackson said that the speed with which poetry _____ overall _____ surprising.

2   Dr Arundell said that Professor Jackson _____ a change as a decline.

3   Sam Henderson stated that the decline _____ in the number of people but in the number of times people _____ poetry readings.

4   Dr Arundell argued that if poetry lovers _____ a wide range of cultural interests, then cinema or theatre goers _____ also have a wide range of interests.

> **Exam tip:** In the IELTS Reading, speakers' opinions are often introduced with a reporting verb, for example: *Mr Stevenson claimed that...*, *Doctors advised that...*, Make sure you identify these reporting verbs to help you understand the opinions better.

Exam practice: Reading – True/False/Not given

Read the following text and answer the questions below.

Protecting the world's culture – the role of museums

For many hundreds of years people have been taking cultural artifacts from foreign countries and keeping them in their own national museums. These objects, which are often items of great value, have been bought, sold, stolen and found for a variety of reasons connected with war, exploration and scientific discovery but the question of ownership still remains.

The ownership argument has two well defined sides, one of which concerns resources and the other cultural heritage. Those who claim museums have a role to play state that objects can be better protected and conserved by well-funded museums in developed countries than in the countries of origin and that they should be allowed to keep objects obtained from abroad. As archaeologist Irene Havers argues, 'these museums have the finance and the academic expertise to ensure that ancient objects are preserved for future generations.' In addition, the major world museums are generally located in capital cities which attract a vast number of tourists. Even if people are not regular museum attendees, tourists will often visit famous museums as part of a sight-seeing trip. This enables museums to generate income in order to maintain their collections.

The opposing view argues that it is important for nations to own their cultural heritage and that museums should return foreign artifacts to the country of origin so that their citizens can learn from them. As Dr Philips from Caledonian University notes, 'having cultural artifacts in national museums is an excellent way to promote learning about history and national identity.' He believes that museums have a duty to return objects to their country of origin in order to allow research to be contained within a culture. He argues that 'foreign researchers may sometimes miss something important because they are studying objects from a culture which they are not part of.' However, Irene Havers asserts that many objects are so old and important that they should only be handled by experienced experts. As she states, 'the value of these objects is immense and museum experts have a responsibility to ensure their care.'

In conclusion, this argument is likely to continue for some time as it encompasses a range of complex, interconnected issues including tourism, academic research, identity and international relations.

QUESTIONS 1-5

Do the following statements agree with the information given in the reading passage? Write:

TRUE	*if the statement agrees with the passage*
FALSE	*if the statement contradicts the passage*
NOT GIVEN	*if there is no information on this in the passage*

1   Museums in developed countries have better financial resources for preserving cultural objects. _____

2   The majority of tourists visit museums in famous capital cities. _____

3   Some academics believe that cultural artifacts should be given back to their country of origin for educational purposes. _____

4   Dr Philips said that researchers always misunderstood foreign cultures. _____

5   According to Irene Havers, only experts are able to categorize ancient, valuable objects. _____

16 Health and fitness

When we speak or write we often want to give more information about something that we have already mentioned. It is important that the listener or reader always knows what we are speaking or writing about, so we use reference words such as *he, it, them*.

Personal pronouns:

We use personal pronouns to refer back to <u>a person or thing</u> which has already been mentioned.
Subject pronouns are: *I, you, she, he, it, we, they*
Object pronouns are: *me, you, her, him, it, us, them*

<u>My mother</u> phoned to say <u>she</u> was ill.	I have a very good <u>personal trainer</u> and I like him.

Note: It is a common pronoun to use in writing and can be used in place of other pronouns such as *this* or *that* for ideas or sentences (with no noun following).

Possessive pronouns:

We use possessive pronouns to refer back to <u>a possession</u> of a person or thing which has already been mentioned.
Possessive pronouns are: *mine, yours, hers, his, ours, theirs*

Note: We do not use *its* as a possessive pronoun.

Your <u>eyesight</u> is much better than <u>mine</u>. (=my eyesight)	I did a <u>fitness test</u> with my friends, Anna and Charlotte. I passed mine but they failed <u>theirs</u>. (=fitness test)

This/that and these/those:

This usually refers to something close to you in distance or time; *that* is generally thought of as further away. Sometimes these words can be used interchangeably.

Regular exercise is essential in burning calories. <u>This/That</u> means people must exercise if they want to lose weight.

We use *this* or *that* to refer back to singular nouns or objects which have already been mentioned. We use *these* or *those* to refer back to plural nouns or objects which have already been mentioned.

'The sports centre has a new <u>climbing wall</u>.' – '<u>That</u> sounds interesting.'	The body has clear <u>daily rhythms</u> and <u>these</u> are disrupted by shiftwork.

We use *this* and *that* to refer back to <u>ideas or whole sentences</u> that have already been mentioned. We can also use *this/that* + noun such as *problem*, *issue*, *aspect*, *view*, *event* to give more information.

<u>Healthcare is directly related to people's ability to work</u>. <u>This</u> issue should be discussed more by the government.	<u>All children should do sport at school</u>. <u>That</u> would help alleviate obesity levels.

Such (such + noun):

We use *such* to refer back to something similar that has already been mentioned.

The company's <u>cholesterol-lowering drug</u> made it the premier marketer of <u>such medicines</u>.

Time and place:

We use *then* and *there* to refer back to a time or place that has already been mentioned.

I go to the <u>gym</u> on Wednesdays and I meet my friend <u>there</u>.	People used to be healthier <u>50 years ago</u> because jobs were more physical <u>then</u>.

Practice exercises

1   **Decide on the correct reference word to complete the sentences. There may be more than one correct answer.**

   1   You should exercise three times a week to maintain _____ fitness.
   2   Long distance runners focus on building up _____ stamina so they can run marathons.
   3   Heart disease is one of the most serious diseases in the world. _____ can be prevented by adopting a healthier lifestyle.
   4   Muscle injuries are very common in athletes. _____ sometimes end an athlete's career.
   5   Vitamin C is essential for optimal health. We can find _____ in fruit and vegetables.
   6   The government spends a considerable amount of money on smoking related diseases. _____ money should be spent on preventing smoking.
   7   My boss has asked the employees to create a company football team. _____ thinks that _____ will help build teamwork.
   8   Many sports people turned professional at the turn of the twentieth century. However, fitness was not a focus of early professional sports people _____.

   > **Listening tip:** It can be difficult to hear reference words because they are short, but they are often important to understand how information about a topic is connected.

2 Complete the spaces in the text below with the correct referencing words. Then listen and check your answers.

Jeanette: Good morning everyone and welcome to my weekly show about fitness. Today I want to talk about ways you can improve (1) _____ fitness without having to join a gym or sports centre. Now first of all, it is important to decide what you want to achieve. Many people want to improve (2) _____ health in general, but other people want to focus on losing weight. I use a combination of both strength building and weight loss exercise to maintain (3) _____ fitness level but I know a couple who go walking twice a week to maintain (4) _____. The most important thing is to do something you like, for example, martial arts, hiking, tennis or watersports. (5) _____ are all good as cardiovascular exercise and strength training. One excellent way is to join a local club because you will meet other people with the same interests as (6) _____. It is also important to keep up motivation levels and exercising with other people can be a good way to do (7) _____. And don't forget about the local park. (8) _____ is a great place to exercise for free. Sometimes parks provide a running track or other communal facilities, all of which are free to use.

3 Read the following extracts from student essays for Writing Task 2 and correct the mistakes in the use of reference words.

1 In my opinion politicians should listen to the people that vote for they. People want to buy healthy food but it is expensive so them buy fast food instead which is not good for his health. Politicians should change it situation.

2 Dieticians suggest vitamins are necessary to combat allergies. It view has been criticized by scientists who say that this nutrients do not always help to reduce allergies. Therefore, because them don't agree, people don't know what advice to follow.

3 Organic food is not a solution to the health problems of the world. Its is less efficient than other methods of food production. In addition, that problems are more often related to less wealthy families in developing countries. Families who live then cannot afford to buy organic produce so they is not useful for us.

4 Read the paragraphs from an IELTS Writing Task 2 and write the noun, sentence or idea that the underlined reference word matches. The first one has been done for you.

What are the causes and effects of obesity and how does it affect society?

One of the largest causes of obesity is the rising cost of food over the years. Although nowadays many supermarkets claim that (1) <u>they</u> provide low cost food, fruit and vegetables have increased considerably in price. (2) <u>This</u> means that it is more difficult for low income families to feed their children fresh, healthy food. As a result, we have seen a rise in obesity and other health related problems. (3) <u>These issues</u> have negative effects on healthcare and education. For example, my mother worries that (4) <u>she</u> will not be able to cook healthy meals for her family if food costs continue to increase.

Another cause is the fact that many young people do not know how to cook. Their parents have not taught (5) them the basic cooking skills. Learning (6) these would help improve young people's knowledge of nutrition. Cooking is not difficult, in fact (7) it can be fun! At the moment, often when young people leave home all (8) they do is eat processed meals. (9) These do not contain enough nutrition and have too much fat and sugar. Unfortunately many people in modern society have become addicted to (10) them.

1 they   = supermarkets   6 these   = _____
2 This   = _____   7 it   = _____
3 These issues = _____   8 they   = _____
4 she   = _____   9 These   = _____
5 them   = _____   10 them   = _____

Exam practice: Writing Task 2

Exam tip: In the IELTS Writing Task 2, referencing words are important to make your writing clear for the reader. Make sure you check that your reference words refer to the correct nouns or ideas in your writing so that the reader can understand your meaning.

You should spend about 40 minutes on this task.
Write about the following topic.

People who cause their own illnesses through unhealthy lifestyles and poor diets should have to pay more for health care.

To what extent do you agree or disagree with this opinion?

Give reasons for your answer and include any relevant examples from your own knowledge or experience.

Write at least 250 words.

There is a model answer in the answer key.

17 Fashion

A text contains paragraphs and a paragraph contains sentences. In English a text is divided into paragraphs and each paragraph focuses on one main idea. All the sentences in a paragraph relate to this main idea. Information in a text and a paragraph is organized as follows: general → specific

Types of text organization

Text is organized according to its purpose. For example, if you are describing a process, you will start at the beginning of the process and explain it step by step. If the text is describing problems and solutions it is usual to explain the problems first then provide the solutions. There are a range of text organization types used in IELTS, for example:

For and against discussion:	a presentation of both sides of a common argument or situation
Cause and effect:	an explanation of the causes and effects of a problem or situation
Advantages and disadvantage:	a discussion of the good and bad points of an issue or situation
Giving an opinion:	a presentation of your opinions on a problem or situation

Paragraph organization

A *topic sentence* explains the main idea of a paragraph. It usually comes at the beginning of a paragraph so that reader knows what the paragraph is about. The topic sentence gives general information on the main idea. **The topic sentence does NOT contain details.**

The other sentences in a paragraph add extra information to the main idea presented in the topic sentence. These sentences can be: *explanations*, *details*, *reasons*, *contradictions*, *problems*, *solutions*, *opposite views* etc. **These sentences contain details and extend the main idea in the topic sentence.**

The function of sentences

Each sentence in a paragraph has a function. It must be connected to the sentence before and the sentence after and add information about the main idea in the topic sentence. Linking words (Unit 10) and reference words (Unit 16) help to connect sentences together and highlight their role.

> **1** Celebrities have had a large impact on the fashion industry. **2** This is due to the fact that they make successful advertising campaigns. **3** Sports stars, pop stars and actors, for example, are often connected with a particular product. **4** Consequently, fans of the celebrity buy the product and company profits increase. **5** However, using celebrities makes people want products they do not want or need.

1 Topic sentence	**3** Example	**5** Problem
2 Reason/explanation	**4** Result	

Practice Exercises

1   **Match following paragraph sentences to their functions.**

   1   During the 1960s fashion in the West went through an extensive transformation.

   2   Most of the changes were due to the influence of popular music and the ideas of young people.

   3   The new less traditional views of lifestyle were seen in items of clothing such as the miniskirt and the choice of bright colours, which became popular with young people.

   4   In contrast, people from the older generation saw this new fashion as undermining traditional values.

   5   This conflict over fashion between the younger and older generations has continued since then.

   A Result   **C** Opposite view   **E** Example

   B Reason   **D** Topic sentence

2   **The text below is from an IELTS Writing Task 1. Look at the graph, divide the text into three paragraphs and then label the function of each paragraph.**

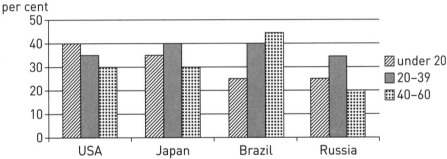

Percentage of yearly income spent on the clothes by age group and nationality.

The bar chart shows the percentage of their income that different age groups spend on clothing in a year. The age groups are children and teenagers, young adults and middle aged people, and the data is from four countries. /Overall, we can see that the 20–39 age group spends the largest part of their income, between 35 and 40 per cent on clothes. In contrast, the group which spends the least on clothes is the oldest group who are between 40 and 60 years old except for in Brazil where this age group spends the most on clothing. / Regarding nationality, in the USA it can be seen that the expenditure on clothes decreases with age, whereas in Brazil this trend is reversed. In Japan and Russia the distribution of spending across the age groups is proportionally similar but for all age groups the Japanese spend more than the Russians.

Functions

A Gives an overall trend and additional details on age groups.

B Provides an introduction to what information is in the graph.

C Gives the overall trends for different nationalities.

3   **Decide which heading A, B or C correctly describes the main idea in each paragraph.**

1   Fashion is often described as a statement of individuality. Despite the fact that many people believe that they have a neutral approach to fashion, the selection of brands and specific items of clothing can reveal a lot about a person's image. An example of this is people who do not buy designer clothes but purchase designer glasses. As a functional accessory it seems unnecessary to purchase designer glasses. Fashion experts claim that this occurs primarily because these people have to wear glasses so they want to make themselves stand out through their glasses choice although they do not apply this to their clothing choices.

     A   Why designer glasses are more important than designer clothes.

     B   Expert advice for choosing designer glasses.

     C   How exclusive items can be used as a personal fashion statement.

2   There are many benefits to the wearing of uniforms at school. Firstly, it reduces the likelihood of children being able to guess the social and financial standing of their classmates. This can help manage bullying in schools, which is often directed at children from lower income families. By wearing uniforms children are less able to display their wealth or ability to purchase fashionable clothing. As a result, there is more chance of children receiving more equal treatment from their peers and staff.

     A   School uniforms make differences in family income less noticeable

     B   The wearing of uniforms reduces some common problems in school.

     C   Wearing uniforms stops children buying fashionable clothes.

3   Nowadays very few of the clothes available in shops are handmade. This is primarily because of the increased labour costs associated with manual work compared to the efficient processing and production of modern machinery. The average factory machine can produce fifty times more garments than a human in the same length of time. That is why the quantity of handmade clothes has decreased considerably. However, making clothes by hand can be profitable since the expertise of designers, dressmakers and pattern cutters is reflected in the price of the goods.

     A   The survival of handmade goods in the face of technology.

     B   How the efficiency of modern factories has harmed handmade production.

     C   The rising production costs of handmade and factory goods.

Exam practice: Reading – matching headings

Choose the correct heading for sections A–E from the list of numbered headings below the following Reading passage.
Write the correct number **i – viii** next to Sections **A–E**.

Section A _____

Fashion is said to have a language that can be read like a text. It serves as an explanation of people's character, personality, lifestyle and values. It works by using signs and codes which are recognisable to others and transmit messages. These signs, codes and messages are called semiotics and influence all aspects of our daily lives. Semiotics in fashion works to convey our identity and in this way messages can be projected to the outside world.

Section B _____

The earliest types of clothing were body painting and adornments. According to experts it is generally believed that the aim of these alterations was to modify the body in some way in order to communicate a specific message. In modern times the aim is largely the same, although the messages are more varied, complex and wide ranging. Nowadays it is common for people to use clothing, colour, fabric, jewellery, hairstyles and even tattoos. Dr Walker from The Centre for Fashion Studies asserts that how we style our bodies is one of the most important factors in defining the self.

Section C _____

Fashion is not only used to define the self but also is a powerful tool for group identity. This can be most clearly seen in youth fashion which is often given a name to help convey the messages of its members. Fashion styles such as goth, mod and emo have semiotic signs and symbols which can represent values, beliefs and political ideologies. Often these values and ideas bring young people together who use clothing as a way to identify others who share their philosophy of life.

Section D _____

On the other hand the semiotics of fashion can be seen as a product of a consumer-based society where appearance, especially through clothing, is valued and judged. This leads to people making conclusions about others on the basis of what they wear. These conclusions are often incorrect and damaging as they attach values and characteristics to people which they may not actually believe in or possess.

Section E _____

In conclusion fashion can be a useful way to analyse an individual, group, society or time period. Clothing and body adornment can highlight status, mood, ideas and values. Although semiotics has sometimes been criticized as a tool of judgment for appearance, it has generally offered a valuable insight into human thought and behaviour throughout history.

i   Connecting fashion and character

ii   Fashion as a tool for unifying people

iii Fashion is a like a language

iv   The effect of consumerism on fashion

v   Using fashion to develop cultural knowledge

vi   Explaining fashion with signs

vii The difference between individual and group identity in fashion

viii Fashioning the body for communication

18 Film and entertainment

Academic language often uses **the passive voice**. The passive is used for the following reasons:

To focus on who/what receives the action

ACTIVE SENTENCE:	Elton John <u>partly wrote</u> *The Lion King* soundtrack.
PASSIVE SENTENCE:	*The Lion King* soundtrack <u>was partly written</u> by Elton John.

In the passive sentence the important focus is on *The Lion King*. Here, the text around this sentence is more likely to be about *The Lion King*. In the first sentence, the text is more likely about Elton John.

When who/what does the action is unimportant or irrelevant

ACTIVE SENTENCE:	<u>The film company released Star Wars</u> in 1977.
PASSIVE SENTENCE:	<u>Star Wars was released</u> in 1977.

Who released the film is unimportant and irrelevant to the message.

To avoid saying who is doing the action

ACTIVE SENTENCE:	In *The Bank Robber*, <u>Harry Flint stole $2bn dollars</u> from a bank.
PASSIVE SENTENCE:	In *The Bank Robber*, <u>$2bn dollars are stolen</u> from a bank.

Here, if the active subject is used (*Harry Flint*), we will reveal the plot of the film.

Forming the passive
Only verbs with an object can be turned into the passive.

An active sentence:
> *The film producers invested $20 million in <u>the promotion</u> of the film.*
> = **a subject** (*The film producers*) + **a verb** (*invested*) + **an object** (*$20million*)

The *subject does* the action and the *object receives* the action.

A passive sentence:
If we want to focus on the amount of money, the passive sentence is as follows:
> *$20million was invested in the promotion of the film (by the film producers).*

Here the object becomes the subject and we add a form of the verb *to be* + past participle (for the continuous form: *to be* + *being* + past participle). See the grammar reference for all forms. Often the active subject becomes unnecessary.
Here you can see the changes:

~~The film producers~~ invested <u>$20 million</u> in the promotion of the film.

was

Other Passive Constructions (avoiding using the subject)

When we don't want to say it is **our opinion**, which is a common technique in academic writing, we often use the passive. Additionally, to avoid using *they* or *people* the passive can be used with reporting verbs.

ACTIVE SENTENCE:	People say that filmmaking is a lucrative industry.
PASSIVE SENTENCE:	Filmmaking is said to be a lucrative industry.

Note: *It is said that filmmaking is a lucrative industry.* is also possible.

See page 123 in the Grammar reference for more information.

Practice Exercises

1   Change the following active sentences into passive sentences. Leave out the active subject if possible.

1   To a certain extent, the entertainment industry is dictating popular culture.

_____

2   People should avoid the new Broadway play *Star Memories*.

_____

3   In the USA, people have voted cinema-going as the most popular weekend hobby.

_____

4   People know that the entertainment industry is very competitive.

_____

5   People regard Hollywood as the most influential town for filmmaking.

_____

6   At the beginning of the 20th century, large film companies contractually restricted famous actors and actresses.

_____

7   In relation to the plot of the book, someone had changed the ending of the film.

_____

8   Someone told us to sit in seats 4a and 4b.

_____

2   Listen to the lecture on the Australian Film Institute. Complete the sentences 1–5 with no more than three words and/or a number from the recording.

1   The Australian Film Institute _____ in 1958.

2   The AFI is _____ for its prestigious awards ceremony.

3   The awards have been raising _____ of the film Industry in Australia since the 1960s.

4   In 1986, _____ included in the AFI awards.

5   The _____ was held at Melbourne's Princess Theatre.

> **Grammar tip:** When talking about the plot of a story or film, use the present tense.

3 In this Speaking Part 2 long turn answer, the student is speaking about her favourite book. She has made some mistakes in her grammar. Read the script and correct the mistakes. Then listen to Track 30 on the CD and check your answers.

'My favourite book is called the *Hunger Games*. It was wrote by Suzanne Collins I think and it is a really good book. The story is set in North America, but at a time when things are very bad. It's a story of a terrible society, which separated into districts. A boy and girl from each district send to take part in the Hunger Games. These games are televised for everyone to see. The games are basically a fight to the death for the children taking part. The story follows a girl called Katniss, who forced to take part in the games when she offers herself up instead of her sister. I like the story so much because it is very exciting. At first, I found it really horrifying, but the more I read it, the more I couldn't put the book down. I really came to like the main character too. She is so strong. I was recommend this book by some friends and it didn't disappoint me.'

4 Below is the prompt for the Part 2 Speaking above. Which part of the prompt did the student **not** answer? _____

Think about your own answers to the prompt and note down some ideas.

> *Describe a book that you've particularly enjoyed. You should say:*
> - *What the book is about*
> - *The main themes in the book*
> - *What the characters are like*
> *and explain why you liked the book.*

What is your favourite book?

_____

_____

What is the book about?

_____

_____

What are the main themes in the book?

_____

_____

What are the characters like?

_____

_____

Why did you like the book?

_____

_____

> **Exam tip:** Make sure you answer <u>all</u> parts of the Part 2 prompt that you receive. This means you will complete the task properly and make better use of the time.

Exam Practice: Speaking Part 2

Read the following prompt for an IELTS Speaking exam Part 2. Give yourself one minute to prepare and make notes. Then speak for two minutes on the topic.

> *Describe a film that you particularly liked. You should say:*
> - *What it is called*
> - *What it is about*
> - *Why you like it*
> *and explain what types of people would like the film.*

Now listen to Track 31 on the CD for the model answer.

31   Make some notes on how you could improve your answer based on the model answer.

19 Wildlife

The zebras which are next to the lake are a new addition to our safari park.

The zebras, which are next to the lake, are a new addition to our safari park.

Defining relative clauses

A defining relative clause is used to give **essential** information about the person, place or thing. Without the defining relative clause the sentence does not have enough meaning, for example:

Animals are called wild animals.

This sentence does not have enough information because not all animals are called wild animals.

Animals <u>which live in a non-domesticated environment</u> are called wild animals.

The relative clause here gives the sentence meaning. We now know **which** animals.

Defining relative clauses are often used in definitions (for example the clause above defines wild animals).

Relative pronouns for defining relative clauses: *who* (person, subject), *whom* (person, object) *which* (thing), *whose* (possessive). Also *when* (time), *where* (place), *why* (after the word *reason*) can be used. *That* can be used in place of the above relative pronouns (except *whose*) in defining relative clauses.

Non-defining relative clauses

A non-defining relative clause is used to give **extra** information about a person, place or thing. The sentence would have enough meaning without the clause and the clause is not necessary. A non-defining relative clause is enclosed by commas.

Penguins<u>, which have tightly packed feathers to keep them warm,</u> live in cold climates.

The clause does not qualify which penguins; it just gives more information about penguins. The sentence *Penguins live in cold climates.* is acceptable alone.

Relative pronouns for non-defining relative clauses: *who* (person, subject), *whom* (person, object) *which* (thing), *whose* (possessive). Also *when* (time), *where* (place) can be used.

Note: That cannot be used as a relative pronoun for non-defining relative clauses.

Subject and object relative pronouns

Relative clauses usually begin with a relative pronoun. The relative pronoun acts as the subject or object of the clause.

Subject relative clauses do not need a new subject as the pronoun acts as the subject:

Jacob is the only person who can feed the lions.

Who is the subject of the relative clause. (Jacob can feed the lions)

Object relative clauses need a new subject as the pronoun represents the object:

The penguins were the best animals that I saw at the zoo.

That refers to *penguins*, so we must add a subject (*I*) for the relative clause (I saw the penguins at the zoo).

Shortening relative clauses

The following are ways in which a relative clause can be reduced:

1 A relative pronoun + verb can be replaced with a participle:

The cat spits at anyone who approaches it. = The cat spits at anyone approaching it.

2 For passive constructions, the relative pronoun + verb *to be* can be removed to leave the past participle:

The man who was injured in the tiger attack went to hospital.

3 With **defining** relative clauses, the relative pronoun can be removed if it is an object pronoun:

Some biologists begin to love the animals that they study.

Practice Exercises

1 **Look at the following sentences and add relative pronouns and punctuation if needed.**

   1 The animal liberation league _____ opinion was criticized by senior politicians failed to get their views acted upon.
   2 Wildlife in Mexico _____ has flourished for many years is now under attack by the industrialization of natural habitats.
   3 Flightless birds are birds _____ cannot fly.
   4 Dian Fossey _____ died in 1985 helped save the mountain gorilla from extinction.
   5 London _____ a third of the city is actually open space is home to a wide variety of wildlife.
   6 An animal _____ sleeps during the day is called 'nocturnal'.
   7 The wildlife photos _____ my sister took in Borneo were the best photos I had ever seen.
   8 Evolution _____ is the generally accepted theory of how life on earth developed is still disputed by some.

   Which one of the above sentences could have the relative pronoun omitted? _____

2 Look at the following questions which may be asked in an IELTS Part 3 Speaking exam. Complete the spaces with the clauses below.

that have no laws to protect their animals

which don't have shops to buy food

that keep animals in small cages

which have been destroyed by industries

that give the animals space to move and look after them well

, which are one of the most endangered rainforest species,

, when the main purpose is enjoyment,

Are zoos cruel to animals?

I don't know. I think some zoos are cruel, for example zoos (1) _____.
But there are also zoos (2) _____. This I think is good. Zoos can also help protect endangered species, and this is a really great thing. There are some countries (3) _____ – that's a real problem. So overall I don't think zoos are as bad as people think.

Do you think we could do more to protect our wildlife?

Yes, we could do a little more. I think many areas of rainforest (4) _____ really need to be rejuvenated. Lots of wildlife live there and if they don't have these forests, they won't be able to survive. Gorillas (5) _____ are dying out rapidly.

Do you think hunting is justified?

I think hunting sometimes is a necessary thing. But I think hunting as a sport (6) _____ is a little cruel. We all need to eat, and societies (7) _____ _____ need to be able to hunt for food. This is necessary for them to be able to live.

🎧 **32** Listen and check your answers. Can you think of any additional points to add to these answers?

> **Grammar tip:** It is important to know which type of relative clause to use (defining or non-defining). This tells you whether you need to punctuate the clause, what pronouns you can use, and if the clause can be shortened. Remember, speakers will pause at commas in non-defining relative clauses. This means that you can identify a defining and non-defining relative clause by the way it is said.

🎧 **3**
33 Using the tip above, listen to the sentences below and decide whether they contain defining or non-defining relative clauses. Punctuate the non-defining relative clauses.

1 Owls are divided into two groups which are classified 'typical owls' and 'barn owls'.
   _____

2 Barn owls which are nocturnal fly silently. _____

3 Owls which are nomadic rear a great number of young. _____

4 Long-eared owls which live in the north migrate to Europe for winter.
   _____

Exam tip: When you hear a relative clause in listening for notes or labels (e.g. a diagram-labelling question), you will normally need to complete it in note form. This will usually mean that the pronoun and any auxiliary verbs are omitted.

 4   Now listen to Track 34 on the CD and complete the diagram with *no more than three words and/or a number*. Notice how the information is given in varied forms of relative clause.

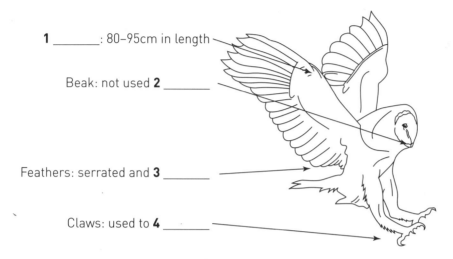

1 _____: 80–95cm in length

Beak: not used **2** _____

Feathers: serrated and **3** _____

Claws: used to **4** _____

Exam practice: Listening – labelling a diagram

 *Complete the diagram below. Write **NO MORE THAN THREE WORDS AND/OR A NUMBER** for each answer.*

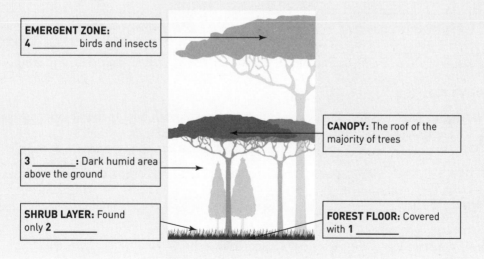

EMERGENT ZONE:
4 _____ birds and insects

CANOPY: The roof of the majority of trees

3 _____: Dark humid area above the ground

SHRUB LAYER: Found only **2** _____

FOREST FLOOR: Covered with **1** _____

20 Men and women

A noun phrase gives extra information about the subject or object of a sentence. The extra information in a noun phrase can come before and/or after the main noun as follows:

Determiner/quantifier + adjective(s) + **NOUN** + prepositional phrase + relative clause

> The recent **increase** of female graduates who have studied technical subjects...

The = determiner / *recent* = adjective / **increase** = noun / *in female graduates* = prepositional phrase / *who have studied technical subjects* = relative clause

Noun phrases can contain one, some or all of these parts.

It is important to notice where the noun phrase begins and ends in a sentence to help you understand what the sentence means. The way to do this is to find the verb in the sentence; everything before the verb is the subject noun phrase and everything that comes after the verb is the object noun phrase.

> The recent increase in female graduates who have studied technical subjects <u>has changed</u> the modern job market.

(noun phrase & subject) + (verb in the singular form because it agrees with *increase*) + (noun phrase & object)

The/an + general noun + specific noun

The general noun describes the category and the specific noun tells us more about the category.

the development of scientific analysis	the pattern of marriage statistics
an approach of primary school teachers	the number of male arts students

Relative clauses

The relative clause provides details which focuses the subject/noun. In the phrase *the men who make the operational decisions* we know exactly which group of men.

the experts who advised the government	figures that support the doctors' claims

Multiple nouns

Some noun phrases are composed of a series of two or more nouns. In the noun phrase *female business owners* all the words are nouns which together form one specific meaning.

community support workers	women government officials

Practice exercises

1   Underline the noun phrase in the following sentences and name the elements
     (determiner/quantifier, adjective, noun, prepositional phrase, relative clause) in it.

     *Example: The / latest / statistics / on gender equality / in the workplace show that in general
     women receive lower pay than men.* = determiner + adjective + noun + prepositional
     phrase + prepositional phrase

     1   A large audience of dedicated fans went to the world championships.
     2   The politician who had proposed new laws on paternity rights won the election.
     3   The development of language skills in boys and girls interests psychologists.
     4   The latest figures from the Driving Standards Agency state that women cause fewer
             accidents.
     5   Gender intelligence stereotypes have changed in recent decades.
     6   Men who decide to give up work to bring up their children are in the minority.

2   **Put the noun phrases from the brackets into the correct order to fit the following text.**

     Throughout history there have been many famous male inventors but less is known
     about female inventors. Interestingly, women have played an increasingly important role
     in invention as they have had wider access to education and employment. In fact, (1) (*of
     household products / that we use in our daily lives / a large quantity*) has been invented by
     women. Some examples include disposable diapers, (2) (*a / computers / for programming /
     language*) and windscreen wipers. In the past (3) (*of women / scientific / the / education /
     and technical*) was limited compared to men but (4) (*who are studying and working in science
     and technology / in the number of women / a dramatic rise*) has occurred in recent years.
     Therefore it can be argued that (5) (*the importance of / which allows people to develop their
     skills / a focused education*) should not be underestimated in the field of invention.

     > **Grammar tip:** Multiple nouns such as *female business owners* can be difficult to order.
     > When trying to order these types of nouns remember that the first noun will describe or
     > categorize the nouns that follow. In this case *business owners* is a noun phrase and we
     > use *female business owners* to state what type of business owners.

3   **In the following paragraph, rewrite the underlined sections as noun phrases. Use the
     structure *the* + general noun + specific noun. You may need to think of a suitable general
     noun. The first one has been done for you.**

     Parents can have different views about (1) how their children are educated at primary
     school depending on whether the child is a boy or girl. Men often think about aspects such
     as (2) what different activities the boys and girls will do, or (3) what space is available for
     doing physical exercise in the school grounds, whereas women can be more concerned
     about (4) how many children will be in the same class as their child and (5) what kind
     of person the teacher is. However, there are many points which concern both parents
     irrespective of gender, for example, (6) how much money a school spends on facilities and
     the quality of care which is provided by the staff.

1 the education of their children

2 _____

3 _____

4 _____

5 _____

6 _____

4 Choose some of the following noun phrases and use them to write a short one-paragraph answer for the essay title below. You can adapt the noun phrases to fit your ideas.

> _Men are more suited to working in fields such as engineering and business whereas women are more suited to the caring professions, for example, nursing or teaching._
>
> _How far do you agree with this statement?_

Noun phrases

the types of job which are more suited to men

women who work in the caring professions

the amount of women working in engineering

men who chooses to become a teacher

the range of employment opportunities for women

women who hold senior positions in business

the increase in female engineers

professions which require a caring personality

the skills needed for working in business

the type of person

_____

_____

_____

_____

_____

Compare your paragraph with the model answer in the answer key.

> **Exam tip:** Noun phrases are widely used in written texts so you need to be able to recognize them in the reading texts and you should try to write them in Tasks 1 and 2 of the Writing exam.

Exam practice: Writing Task 2

You have 40 minutes to answer the following essay question.

Write about the following topic:

> Women are better at childcare than men therefore they should focus more on raising children and less on their working life.
>
> To what extent do you agree or disagree with this statement?

Give reasons for your answer and include any relevant examples from your own knowledge or experience.

Write at least 250 words.

_____

_____

_____

_____

_____

_____

_____

_____

_____

_____

_____

_____

_____

_____

_____

_____

_____

Compare your essay with the model answer in the answer key.

Audio script

Unit 1   Holidays and travel

Track 01

Examiner: Where do you live?

Nikolas: I come from Moscow. I have lived there for 6 years. My family moved from the countryside when I was 12 years old.

Examiner: Do you still live with your family?

Nikolas: Yes, I do. I live with my parents and share a room with my brother. My brother still goes to school. He is only 8 years old.

Examiner: Do you like Moscow?

Nikolas: Yes, I love Moscow. When I first arrived, I didn't like it much because it was so different, but I have grown accustomed to it. Now, I know my way around and have lots of friends.

Examiner: How has Moscow changed recently?

Nikolas: It has become more international, and more exciting. In the last few years, about ten new international restaurants have opened in my area alone and I often eat in them now with my friends. I have lots of international friends who have come to study at the University in Moscow, and we often meet in the evenings.

Track 02

1   What kinds of holidays do you like?

2   What was the last place you visited on holiday?

3   What kinds of transport do you use regularly?

4   How long have you lived in your home town?

5   Have you travelled to many different places in your country?

Track 03

Examiner: What kinds of holidays do you like?

Student: I like beach holidays because well, I enjoy relaxing and I love the sun. I don't really like city breaks or activity holidays. They're too tiring for me. I work so hard that I like to just do nothing when I'm away. I usually go to Italy on holiday, which is really nice but quite expensive!

Examiner: What was the last place you visited on holiday?

Student: I went to one of the Greek islands last year. I was there for two weeks. I flew there but took the boat back, which was a real treat. I love travelling by boat! When I was there I saw a few sights and ate some of the local food, but mainly I just stayed by the pool and sunbathed.

Examiner: What kinds of transport do you use regularly?

Student: I live in a big city, Shanghai, and so I often use public transport. I go to work by bus which usually takes about thirty minutes. Lots of people in Shanghai travel by bike, but I've never ridden a bicycle because I'm too scared! It sounds ridiculous but it's true! I often visit my parents by train, but last week there was an accident so I took the bus.

Examiner: How long have you lived in your home town?

Student: I've lived here all my life. Although I've worked in lots of different cities, I've never stayed there for more than a few months. I was born in Shanghai and have lived here now for twenty one years. I lived with my parents when I was younger but now I've got a flat on my own in the city centre! It's not very big but it suits me.

Examiner: Have you travelled to many different places in your country?

Student: Yes, I've travelled to lots of different cities in China. I've been to Beijing, Guangzhou, Nanjing, Harbin and Kunming. My favourite one was Beijing. I went there a couple of years ago and it was really fantastic. I didn't realize how cold it was in Beijing. I was amazed. Apparently, it is really hot in the summer but really cold in the winter time. Unfortunately, I went in the winter!

Unit 3 Fame

Track 04

Presenter: In today's programme I'll continue examining the impact of fame on lifestyle using the style icon Gloria Van Broncken as an example. Before becoming famous in the modelling industry, Gloria had lived in a small village and had never travelled outside her own country. She used to work in a clothes store and she enjoyed all the usual activities of a teenager in her free time. She'd been working in the clothes store for two years when a customer who represented a model agency spotted her and signed her up. By the time she was 21 Gloria had travelled round the world several times and had appeared on the cover of many international fashion magazines. Now the impact of such drastic lifestyle changes can be very significant ... (*fade*)

Unit 4 Education

Track 05

Librarian: Hello there. How can I help you?

John: I'm going to do a presentation on Mary Shelley, and I'd like to get some books on her.

Librarian: Okay. The biographies are on the third floor. I'll write the aisle number down for you.

John: Thanks. I might use the Internet too and look for resources on there.

Librarian: That's a good idea. If you're going to use the Internet, have a look on the Great British Authors website.

John: Thanks, I will. I haven't heard of that site before. Thanks very much for the information.

Librarian: That's quite all right. Feel free to come and ask me any questions and I will do my best to help.

Track 06

Andy:	Hi, is this the Student Affairs Office?
Carol:	Yes, it is. I'm Carol. How can I help you?
Andy:	Hi, I'm Andy. Well, I'm new at the University and I was told I needed to come here to complete my registration?
Carol:	You're in the right place yes.
Andy:	Great!
Carol:	Firstly, do you know your way around the campus?
Andy:	No, it's my first day. I'm going to explore later.
Carol:	Well, hold on, I'll give you a map of the University. Errmm... they're just...
Andy:	There are some over there on the wall. I'll grab one.
Carol:	Thanks, sorry about that. Have you organized your tour around the main library?
Andy:	No, not yet. I'm going to go to the library later to do it.
Carol:	I'll do it for you here. There is a tour at 4.30 today. Shall I put you on that?
Andy:	Yes, please that'd be great! I'm going to complete the New Student Form later on today. Do I bring that to you?
Carol:	You can't complete it yourself. You'll need to go to the main administration office as one of the staff members there needs to fill the form out for you. It's just by the main hall, you can't miss it. You can get a visa form from them too, but you'll need to send the confirmation yourself once you've completed the form.
Andy:	I don't need a visa, so I should be okay with that, but thanks.
Carol:	Okay, can I help you with anything else?
Andy:	Yes, please. There's just so much to do, and I don't know where to go for some things. Could you help me?
Carol:	Yes, of course. It's a bit daunting when it's all new.
Andy:	Well, at the moment I'm staying in a bed and breakfast. I left it a bit late to get some accommodation! But I'd like a place of my own. Do you know where I can find information about places I could rent?
Carol:	Good job you asked! Lots of people go to the Administrative Department and then get sent back here to Student Affairs! Here's the latest list of accommodation!
Andy:	Wow that was easy. And where can I get information on my rental agreement?
Carol:	Well you need to find a place first before you get it checked, but I'll do it when you've found somewhere.
Andy:	Great. I'm going to register with the doctor later on at the Admin Department. Do they also have information on the area?
Carol:	You'll need to go to Student Support to get a doctor, not Admin. They also have everything you need to know about the town. They're really helpful. The Admin Department is really only there for official things such as visa regulations, loans and paying for your course.
Andy:	Okay. Great. There's so much to remember!
Carol:	There certainly is, but once you're settled in it will all be much easier. Good luck!
Andy:	Thanks for your help.

Unit 5   The Internet

Track 07

Interviewer: Welcome to the programme, Bob Lamont. Now you're going to talk to us about the online gaming industry. We've had many listeners, especially parents of young children, email questions about the future of the gaming industry and how it's going to develop.

Bob Lamont: Well, hopefully I'll be able to answer some of their questions. Firstly, it's important to remember that this is an industry that develops incredibly rapidly and so it's difficult to make definite predictions. So, in terms of significant developments that people working in the industry are preparing for, the most interesting is the fact that the age group of gamers (people who play online and video games) will change dramatically. We predict that by 2020 the average age range will have shifted from teenagers to the over 50s. This is because in the future young people will be using new forms of entertainment but those who are young now are more likely to continue using the forms of entertainment they are already used to in later life. By 2020 this age group will have been playing the same type of game for half their lives and are unlikely to change.

The types of games will progress too from the platform-based games we have now, which we expect people to be using until 2015, to 3D games towards the end of the decade. However, before everyone is using 3D games there will be a period when networked games will become the dominant format. This is mostly to do with the technology available and the fact that gaming companies won't have invested enough money to make 3D cheap enough for the mass market until at least 2018. Now, as you would expect, the gaming market will spread so that by 2020 companies will have created a worldwide marketing strategy for every game, therefore reducing the need to create new games for different regional markets. This is different from today where we see that the online gaming industry is much more focused on the region of Asia and this is likely to continue for a few more years.

One final point to mention here is the competition from other forms of entertainment. Over the next decade very few forms of entertainment will be able to compete with the gaming industry. However, there is talk of movies becoming interactive in the future. This is a real threat. Tech companies will have developed the necessary technology for interactive movies by 2015 and this may attract gamers who like character-based games in large numbers.

Interviewer: Fascinating, Bob. I didn't realize it was such a complex business. Thank you very much for your insight ... (*fade*)

Track 08

Curator: Good morning ladies and gentlemen and welcome to the Museum of Technology. We'll be taking a tour around the three floors, which will last approximately one hour and then after that you'll be able to explore the museum on your own.

Now, let's begin with The Internet: Past, Present and Future on the first floor. By this Friday the exhibition will have been open for two weeks, it started on

July 10th, and it'll continue for three more weeks so make sure you see it today otherwise it'll probably have finished by the time you think about coming back! The final day of the exhibition is 31st July. The most interesting part of this section of the museum is about the Internet of the future. As you walk around you'll see some large 3D touch screens which show how we'll probably be using computers in about five years. These screens are definitely the best part of the display and something you must see.

Moving on to the third floor, the exhibition here is all about communicating via the Internet and it's called Social Networking. This exhibition is open throughout August from 1st to 30th. There is a fascinating part of the exhibition which is really worth seeing as it compares mobile phone and Internet usage and shows how we'll be using social networking in the future. According to some scientists, by the middle of this century we will have been participating in communication through social networking so much that mobile phones will have become obsolete! Make sure you take a look at the world digital map which shows this visually, as it's quite amazing.

The final exhibition is opening on the fourth floor and is dedicated to small hand-held devices that companies will have introduced into our shops by the end of next year. In fact you may have already seen some of them being advertised on TV. The name of this section is 'Portable Devices of the 21st Century' and it's starting tomorrow on July 22nd and will be open until August 20th. This part of the museum is about sixth sense technology. This technology will have been included in all portable devices like mobile phones and music players within three years or so. It also shows us examples of satellite tracking systems which we will be using to help us plan our daily lives. These two sections are fascinating and I recommend you spend some time viewing both.

So, let's start the tour. If you could all follow me... (*fade*)

Unit 6   The family

Track 09

I'm going to talk about my grandmother on my father's side. She is quite little and has white hair and glasses. I have glasses too. We're the only people in the family that wear glasses! She is very old now and I don't get to see her very often... I think I see her maybe two or three times a year. She lives quite far away in the countryside. It takes us about three hours to travel there. Whenever we visit, she always gives sweets to me. She's important to me because she's so kind and so nice, and I really love her. She's definitely my favourite family member! I think I take after her in some ways. We laugh at the same things and we both like reading. When we go and visit, we always go out walking in the fields and have a really lovely time. My dad always says that we're very similar. I'd like to be as wise as her when I am older. I'd also like to have a similar life. She had a very successful career. She was a doctor and worked for charities. She was very much in love with my grandfather, which I think is lovely.

Unit 8   Food

Track 10

Simon:	Excuse me, my name's Simon and I'm a dietician working here at the University. Would you mind if I asked you some questions? I'm doing a survey for the Students' Union on student eating habits.
Jim:	Oh really.
Simon:	Yes, we're trying to find out how we can improve the meals served in the university canteens and cafes based on what students like to cook for themselves.
Jim:	Right. Well, I've a few minutes before class so yes, I can answer some questions.
Simon:	Thanks a lot. Firstly, what's your name and what course are you studying?
Jim:	I'm Jim and I'm doing Biology.
Simon:	Okay. Now can you tell me how often you eat meat?
Jim:	About once a week. The cost is really high these days so I can't afford to eat much meat.
Simon:	Right. And what about fish and vegetables?
Jim:	I don't like fish so that hardly features in my diet at all, but I often eat vegetables. In fact both at lunchtime and for my evening meal I usually make meals from vegetables as they're quick and easy.
Simon:	Mmm, that's a good idea. Do you think we should have more vegetable dishes in the Students' Union canteens?
Jim:	I think so because price is a big factor for students deciding to be vegetarian. If the university served good quality vegetarian food they could make it cheaper and this might attract more students.
Simon:	Yes, I see your point. Now, how would you evaluate your diet?
Jim:	That's a good question! I know my diet contains far too much sugar. The problem is that I love fizzy drinks like coke and lemonade. I'm pretty sure that that's where most of the sugar comes from. What I really have to do is to try to find a way to stop this and drink some kind of juice or water instead.
Simon:	Yes, you're right, that's what a dietician, nutritionist or doctor would recommend.
Jim:	I know, I know. At the moment I don't drink enough water – on an average day I only have a couple of glasses.

Track 11

Last year I went to a wonderful restaurant overlooking the river in my city, Marseille, with a group of friends. The special occasion was my friend's 21st birthday and we decided to go out for dinner. We wanted to eat beef because this restaurant is famous for meat, but as we arrived late they didn't have any beef left. Instead we ate bouillabaisse which is a kind of seafood stew containing fish and shellfish. I had a couple of glasses of orange juice. For dessert we each had a slice of birthday cake which the restaurant had made especially for my friend. The cake had 21 candles and my friend blew them all out in one go so she made many wishes for the future. We had so much fun that night.

Track 12

I'm going to talk about an English dessert called trifle. This is a dish that people usually eat in summer and it's been very popular since the 1950s. It's made from fruit, cake, custard and jelly and we often eat it with some cream. Trifle is really easy to make because it doesn't actually need cooking. Um first of all, you cut up some cake into slices and then you put the slices of cake into a bowl. Some people like to cover the cake in sherry otherwise it can go a bit hard. Next you need to chop up some fruit but you can't use just any fruit; it must be berries such as strawberries, raspberries or blackberries. After covering the cake with berries, you need to make some jelly and pour this over the fruit. When the jelly has cooled it's time to add custard. You can use a tin of custard but it's better to make your own – people can always tell the difference. Finally, add the cream. It's best to only use a little cream because trifle is quite rich. And then put a few raspberries on the top for decoration. I love it because of the mix of fruit and sweet custard.

Unit 10   Youth

Track 13

As part of this module on youth, today we are going to look at current youth initiatives in the UK. Some of which are more successful than others, I must say. The last government spent a lot of money on setting up initiatives that sadly have been left in desperate need of funding since the new government has come into power.

Firstly, volunteering schemes are incredibly successful in the UK. These schemes are cheap to run, which is a huge benefit. In addition to this, the schemes are community based. This means that the benefits are spread widely throughout each local community. The uptake has doubled in the last ten years and I believe this is an area where more focus should be placed.

Secondly, sports clubs are a huge youth initiative, with more than 20,000 emerging in the last ten years in England alone. Although the numbers are very positive, these schemes are expensive to staff. If these are to continue to flourish, this area will need a significant cash injection.

Lastly, there are a certain number of drama clubs that have emerged in the last ten years. Although it was thought that these would be hugely popular, they have actually attracted only small numbers of students. Moreover, they are costly, and finding a venue for such clubs has proved difficult as many local halls are running at capacity. As a result of these factors, these clubs are not likely to continue in the long term.

To conclude, as we can see, some of the schemes are flourishing, yet many are short of money and other essential resources. In order to enhance the youth experience, the government must identify new schemes which are cost effective, yet enjoyable to teens.

Track 14

So, what other initiatives could the government focus on? Well, due to the success of the sports clubs, new 'open spaces' initiatives are being discussed, for example football tournaments in local playing fields or athletics days in local parks. This could regenerate local areas and renew interest in activities for young people. Staffing would still be necessary, although young people could take an active role in organizing and managing competitions. This could cut down staff costs significantly.

In addition to the open spaces scheme, there has been discussion of reinvigorating the 'taste of work' scheme, which gives young people a chance to get work experience in a variety of jobs in their school holidays. However, this scheme has met with harsh criticism from some politicians who think that it's a way of providing a free workforce by stealth. In fact, I think it is fair to say that this scheme will not see any renewed interest because of these criticisms.

Lastly, the scheme that there has been a lot of talk about is the outward bound activities courses, or OBAC for short. This has been successful in many other countries, such as Canada, Mexico and Brazil. The activity courses give young people a chance to get out into the countryside and enjoy nature. As a result of this, they also give teens a chance to learn life skills and experience adventure on a broader scale.

Unit 11 People and places

Track 15

Examiner: How has the place you live in changed recently?

Student: Well, in my city there is a lot more traffic than there used to be. This is because of the new business centre, which has brought a lot more people to the city for work. This has made the city richer than it was. In fact that's the most significant difference – the city is not as poor as it was 10 years ago.

Examiner: So, you're studying here in Sydney. How is your town or city different from Sydney?

Student: Mm, there are quite a few differences such as the shop opening hours – the shops in Tokyo stay open much later than those here in Sydney. Then there's the transport system which is more efficient and convenient. But the weather is the same as here in Australia.

Examiner: Is it a good place to live?

Student: Yes, it's really nice. I think it's considerably better than other cities in my country because it's more modern. It's also got a lot of parks which I really like and this means that it's not nearly as crowded as some places.

Track 16

James: I think our presentation should focus on why living in the countryside has become more attractive to families nowadays than in the past.

Suzanne: I'm not so sure. Although the statistics Professor Davies showed us in the lecture gave the impression that there are more families moving to the country now than at any time during the last 20 years, he also mentioned that there aren't as many available houses in suburban areas so many families don't have as much choice as before.

Helen: Yes, Suzanne, you're right. Perhaps that's actually more important. People think that the same housing stock exists as in the past, but that's not true. How about we focus our presentation on the fact that the choice of location for families is not as wide as during the 1980s and this is what is affecting the trend of moving to the countryside.

James: Okay. I think you've thought about the presentation a lot more clearly than me.

Helen: Thanks.

Suzanne: I think Helen's right. We want Professor Davies to think that we have done as much research for the presentation as we could and not only used the reading list.

James: Yes, you're right. Otherwise our final grade won't be nearly as good as our last presentation – so we need to read as widely as possible.

Track 17

Alison:	So, Greg, Kirsty, have you done much research for our project yet?
Greg:	I haven't done as much reading as I'd planned to but I've got quite a lot of books and journal articles that might be relevant.
Kirsty:	Good work Greg! I think I might have worked out how we can approach the project and give it a more specific focus than the title that Dr Jones suggested, which is too vague.
Greg:	Oh really – how's that?
Kirsty:	Well, we know that the New Seven Wonders of the World were chosen a few years ago but I think that how they were chosen and what this says about people's relationships to their architectural and natural national heritage is far more interesting than just doing a project that describes what they are and why they were chosen. What do you think Alison?
Alison:	You know I think you could be right there. Didn't Dr Jones mention something in our last lecture about how many more people voted for some of the wonders than the total number of people in the country?
Greg:	Mmm, that did happen. In a sense it wasn't really a voting system at all – more like a TV talent show. It wasn't nearly as scientific as political voting systems because people could vote as many times as they wanted and it was all done via the Internet so it only applied to people with access to a computer. And most of the votes for the wonders came from the country's own citizens.
Kirsty:	Mmm, that's interesting. I think therefore that we can show how the modern choices were different from the original Seven Wonders of the Ancient World because the original wonders were chosen by travellers while the latest list was chosen by people from the same country as the wonder itself. From this we can analyse the choices and how having a building or site on this list could be more advantageous to some countries than others. For example, countries which rely less heavily than others on tourism may not have been nearly as interested in the whole competition as those who wanted to boost visitor numbers. Then we could compare this with how travellers chose the previous wonders.
Alison:	Okay, now I understand and yes I think it's a great idea. Let's do it!
Greg:	Yes, I think that'll really give us an edge compared to the other students. It'll make the final project considerably more original. Remember, Dr Jones isn't expecting much from us given the result for our last project! But I'm just slightly worried that we might not have as much time as we'd like to do the reading.
Alison:	Mmm.... I see what you mean. Well, why don't we do as much reading of these books and journals as we can and then meet again on Friday to make a final decision on content?
Kirsty:	That's a good idea Alison.
Greg:	Absolutely, then we can make sure we won't read too much and will still have enough time for the actual project writing.

Unit 12   Crime

Track 18

Examiner: How can crime be prevented?

Student: Crime prevention must start from education. If people are not raised well, then they might commit crimes in the future. It's the responsibility of both parents and schools to educate children in the difference between right and wrong. This could be done in special ethics classes in schools, and perhaps parenting classes might be a good idea for parents who are unsure of how to raise children with more moral values. These classes shouldn't be compulsory though as this might be too expensive and unnecessary. However, although all parents might not go, it could be useful for those who are struggling. More information could help these parents.

Track 19

1   Why do you think people become criminals?

2   What do you think the role of prisons should be: punishment or rehabilitation?

3   What do you think is the best way to deal with juvenile crime?

4   Do you think people commit crimes because of violence on TV or in video games?

5   Is crime always linked to poverty?

Track 20

Examiner: Why do you think people become criminals?

Student: Errr... because life can be difficult for some people. Crime can present an easy way to get things they want in life. Even though people know they shouldn't do it, the temptation could be very strong, especially if they are in a desperate situation. Although they ought to work hard or get help, sometimes they just can't.

Examiner: What do you think the role of prisons should be: punishment or rehabilitation?

Student: I think prisons should focus on rehabilitation more. This is because those prisoners will one day be back on the streets, and so education might make them better in society. Prisons ought to help solve the problem of crime. I think being in prison is punishment enough and so while people are in prisons, there should be some kind of constructive effort to change their behaviour.

Examiner: What do you think is the best way to deal with juvenile crime?

Student: Young people must have role models. This might prevent some young people getting involved in crime in the first place. Parents have to take responsibility for their children too. In fact, I think parents should be fined if their children commit a crime. I think this might be quite a good answer, as children can't always know right or wrong without their parents telling them.

Examiner: Do you think people commit crimes because of violence on TV or in video games?

Student: No, I don't. People don't have to do what they see on a screen. People have their own minds and can tell the difference between reality or fiction. People can see violence on the news. It doesn't make everyone who watches the news a potential criminal. People who are influenced by games and TV in this way probably have an underlying problem.

Examiner:	Is crime always linked to poverty?
Student:	Not always. Although I think that some crime is because of poverty, there are other factors which we ought to consider. For example, plain greed, laziness, mental illness and personal problems could also contribute to some crimes. We can look at things like crimes of passion or fraud which are not always committed due to poverty as examples.

Unit 13   The planet

Track 21

Kelly:	Hi everyone. So, let's get started on our essay. Mark, have you done the research from last week?
Mark:	Well, yes and no. I was trying to follow up on the suggestions from the lecture and I searched the library for books and journals. But I couldn't find anything relevant to our topic.
Louise:	Well, maybe you were too late. We got the essay title two weeks ago so other students might have taken out all the books already.
Mark:	Yes, I guess so.
Kelly:	It doesn't sound likely to me. All the books couldn't have been taken out – there's lots of books about astronomy in the main library.
Mark:	Well, there was one book but I couldn't borrow it because it's a reference only book.
Kelly:	Mm. We should have started this project earlier. What are we going to do now?
Louise:	The other students must have been very keen to start! Well, don't worry. Why don't we just reserve the books we want? I've found some articles we can start reading now and then we'll be more focused for when the other students return the books we need.

Track 22

Dave:	So Abi, can Helen and I show you our presentation to see if you think it's okay?
Abi:	Of course, no problem.
Helen:	Thanks a lot. Okay first of all, we're going to show the explorers' route on the map here and explain what happened on the expedition by highlighting some key events.
Abi:	Right.
Helen:	And we think it's important to mention that the expedition started quite badly. You see the original base camp had to be moved. The original plan was to start from the tree line at the bottom of the mountain but the explorers couldn't set up camp there because of the rain so they moved higher up.
Dave:	The idea is to highlight the importance of planning in exploratory expeditions. The Robertson team should have known that they couldn't have started from the tree line in the rainy season.
Abi:	Yes, they really should have checked that!
Dave:	In the end the camp was set up on the edge of the snow line. Okay, so moving on, Joan Robertson and her team found several new plant species on the lower slopes of the peak and when they were halfway up the mountain they came across some fossils which they worked out were from dinosaurs.

Abi:	How did they know the fossils were from dinosaurs? Surely they couldn't have identified them so easily whilst on the expedition?
Helen:	But that's the important point. This team were not just explorers but also scientists. In order to make the trip more useful, they took scientific equipment to analyse anything they found so they were able to identify the dinosaur fossils correctly.
Abi:	It's good to make this clear if your project is supposed to be about the importance of scientific expeditions rather than exploratory ones.
Dave:	Absolutely.
Abi:	So am I right to think that the Robertson expedition took longer as a result of the research?
Dave:	Well, they should have taken longer because they were conducting a lot of experiments but modern technology enabled them to do the experiments and reach the summit in under four weeks. In fact they arrived at the top on day 26 of the trip.

Track 23

Andrew:	Hi Penny. Hi Terry. (Hellos) How are you both getting on with your natural disaster essays? I can't believe we all chose the same subject of earthquakes! I've found it really interesting.
Penny:	Yes, it is interesting Andrew, but I could have made the topic narrower. There is so much to cover. It's really hard to organize the information I've found.
Terry:	Ah, but that just gives you more to write about. I'd rather have too much material than not enough! I think Andrew is right. I've found the topic fascinating too!
Penny:	Maybe. I'm not so sure Terry. Andrew, how have you done on the statistics research? That's what you were researching when I last saw you.
Andrew:	It's been interesting, but I had to look really hard for relevant information.
Penny:	But you found some in the end?
Andrew:	Yes, I've got lots of statistics on past earthquakes and where the plates are more unstable.
Penny:	That's great! I've been working on plate movement. I think by adding this to my essay I'll have a really good foundation of how earthquakes come about.
Terry:	I was looking at future earthquake predictions, but I didn't find much information actually. I should have focused more on how earthquakes are scientifically identified and measured. I think that would have been more relevant.
Penny:	That's a shame. Well, why don't we compare some of the information we've found? It might all give us some ideas of what to read next!
Andrew:	Well, it turns out that many earthquakes could have been predicted according to the frequency of past earthquakes in the area.
Terry:	Really, that's not what I found out at all. I think you should go back and check that.
Andrew:	I don't know – maybe I should.
Penny:	Well, my research looks particularly at how convergence and divergence of the plates causes movement of the Earth. We sometimes forget that the planet is not a still object but actually it is constantly moving. This causes things like new seas, mountains, and earthquakes. The whole world is moving! Terry, didn't your research find anything?
Terry:	Unfortunately not. I think I need to research another area as I couldn't see any evidence of earthquakes being predictable.
Andrew:	Well, I can also show you what I've got and maybe that will help.
Terry:	Thanks

Unit 14   Globalization

Track 24

3   Does globalization represent a change in the way people view the world?

4   Should globalization be controlled by governments?

5   Most global companies are from the West – is this a good or a bad thing?

6   Do you think that globalization helps us to understand different people and cultures?

Track 25

Examiner: How do you think globalization might change the world in the future?

Student: I think that if globalization continues to develop, young people of the future will have a different understanding of things like nationality and culture.

Examiner: Has globalization caused young people to care less about their countries?

Student: I don't think so. If globalization had caused young people to care less about their countries, we wouldn't see so much national pride in sporting competitions like the Olympics or the World Cup.

Examiner: What would you say to someone who thinks that globalization is ruining the world?

Student: I would say that they should be more positive. If globalization didn't exist, we wouldn't have so many opportunities for work or travel and we wouldn't be able to buy so many different products.

Examiner: Can globalization make the world a more equal place?

Student: I think this depends on what you mean by equal. If people in a country have the same opportunities in life, then globalization is good and can help the world but this is not always what happens.

Track 26

Examiner: What are the main disadvantages of globalization?

Student: In my opinion the main disadvantages are for cultures which aren't particularly strong. I think globalization could in fact destroy some small, local cultures. When my parents were young, the local dialect in our town was spoken all the time, but now more and more people in the town are from other countries and our dialect isn't spoken so much. If globalization hadn't transformed the way people move around the world, our town wouldn't have changed so much, and we might still be using our local dialect!

Examiner: Do you think globalization has made the world a better place?

Student: Well, in many ways yes. I think in general people have more knowledge about the world due to globalization. For example, if I hadn't studied in Australia, I wouldn't speak English as well as I do and I wouldn't have lots of friends from around the world.

Examiner: How has globalization changed the way we travel and communicate?

Student: I think it has changed things greatly. The world is a much smaller place than it was, say, 50 years ago. If I wanted to go to the other side of the world, I could get there in a day! That's incredible!... And not only is it easier to travel, we can now communicate with people on the other side of the world instantly through things like virtual messaging and webcams. If we didn't have this kind of progress in travel and communication, we would know a lot less about other cultures, and I think that would be a pity.

Examiner: How has globalization benefited people in your country?

Student: It's made a really big difference to how people in my country see themselves in relation to other countries. And I think that people will see more benefits in the future if they continue to be open-minded about it.

Examiner: What are the consequences of allowing large companies to sell their products all over the world?

Student: I think it's great. I know some people think that it's negative but I don't. I think that everyone should have the opportunity to grow their company. All companies started small but if you make good products, people will buy them. If there'd been strict laws against international trade, the world economy wouldn't have grown as much and everyone would've suffered.

Unit 15   Culture and modern society

Track 27

Well, my best friend once gave me some really good advice when I was younger. I used to worry a lot about my appearance when I was a teenager and it made me feel unconfident. I often thought people were staring at me and thinking that I looked bad. Once, one of my classmates asked me where I had bought my clothes and I thought it was a criticism. My friend told me not to worry about the way I looked. She said that all teenagers felt that way and recommended concentrating on having fun instead. It was quite difficult but I tried to focus more on studying and my hobbies. After a while I felt better and my parents said that I had changed and become more outgoing. I was really pleased with this and as a result my confidence increased even more. So, I think yes I would give this advice to other teenagers. Although it's difficult advice to follow, I think it can really help young people who are going through a hard time. It's really important to be positive and understand that this period of your life involves lots of changes in your personality but that in the end you will feel fine.

Unit 16   Health and fitness

Track 28

Jeanette: Good morning everyone and welcome to my weekly show about fitness. Today I want to talk about ways you can improve your fitness without having to join a gym or sports centre. Now first of all, it is important to decide what you want to achieve. Many people want to improve their health in general, but other people want to focus on losing weight. I use a combination of both strength building and weight loss exercise to maintain my fitness level but I know a couple who go walking twice a week to maintain theirs. The most important thing is to do something you like, for example, martial arts, hiking, tennis or watersports. These are all good as cardiovascular exercise and strength training. One excellent way is to join a local club because you will meet other people with the same interests as you. It is also important to keep up motivation levels and exercising with other people can be a good way to do this. And don't forget about the local park. It is a great place to exercise for free. Sometimes parks provide a running track or other communal facilities, all of which are free to use.

Unit 18   Film and entertainment

Track 29

Thank you for coming to this talk on the Australian Film Institute, or AFI as most of us know it. We pride ourselves on the work we have done over the last 50 years, and I hope to let you know how we will keep promoting and developing this great country's film industry. I'm going to start by giving you a little bit of history about the AFI, then I'll go on to tell you about the work we're involved in at the moment, and then tell you a little bit about what the future holds for the AFI.

So, let's start at the beginning. 1958 is an important date in our history, as it was when the Institute was founded. Since then, we have been working continuously for the following purpose; to promote film and television in Australia. I think however our celebrated film and television awards are what we at the AFI are most well known for, which do indeed fulfil our aims of promotion of the industry. In fact, we think these awards have also elevated the standards of Australian film since their inception in the sixties. We're incredibly proud of them.

The awards became so popular that we expanded them. In 1986, TV categories were added to the list of prestigious awards we offered. The awards have grown in popularity and status over the years, and there is no doubt that we are one of the leading film and television award ceremonies in the country. We have just recently held our 50th anniversary, which took place at Melbourne's Princess Theatre. Some big names in the film and television industry were there and it was a real celebration of success.

Now, this leads me up to our present work...

Track 30

My favourite book is called the *Hunger Games*. It was written by Suzanne Collins I think and it is a really good book. The story is set in North America, but at a time when things are very bad. It's a story of a terrible society, which is separated into districts. A boy and girl from each district are sent to take part in the Hunger Games. These games are televised for everyone to see. The games are basically a fight to the death for the children taking part. The story follows a girl called Katniss, who is forced to take part in the games when she offers herself up instead of her sister. I like the story so much because it is very exciting. At first, I found it really horrifying, but the more I read it, the more I couldn't put the book down. I really came to like the main character too. She is so strong. I was recommended this book by some friends and it didn't disappoint me.

Track 31

A film I saw recently which I particularly liked was *Toy Story 3*. It's the third of a trilogy of *Toy Story* films, and I think it's the best, but saddest one. These films are made by Pixar and they are cartoon films, but I think they are for adults as well as children! The film is about toys that get thrown out as their owner is too old to play with them anymore. They're given to a nursery school, but the nursery school children are horrible and the toys are treated really badly. So, the story follows their journey to get back to their original owner. The main characters in the film are Woody, who is voiced by Tom Hanks, and Buzz Lightyear. I like this film so much because the story and the animation are so good. I found that, even though it's a cartoon, it was really easy to get involved in the characters and what was happening to them. I think I cried for the last half hour of the film... but it's an incredibly heartwarming film about love and friendship. I would recommend this film to anyone who enjoys both a laugh and a cry! I think this film would be loved by most people in the world.

Unit 19　Wildlife

Track 32

Examiner: Are zoos cruel to animals?
Student: I don't know. I think some zoos are cruel, for example zoos that keep animals in small cages. But there are also zoos that give the animals space to move and look after them well. This I think is good. Zoos can also help protect endangered species, and this is a really great thing. There are some countries that have no laws to protect their animals – that's a real problem. So, overall I don't think zoos are as bad as people think.
Examiner: Do you think we could do more to protect our wildlife?
Student: Yes, we could do a little more. I think many areas of rainforest which have been destroyed by industries really need to be rejuvenated. Lots of wildlife live there and if they don't have these forests, they won't be able to survive. Gorillas, which are one of the most endangered rainforest species, are dying out rapidly.
Examiner: Do you think hunting is justified?
Student: I think hunting sometimes is a necessary thing. But I think hunting as a sport, when the main purpose is enjoyment, is a little cruel. We all need to eat, and traditional societies which don't have shops to buy food need to be able to hunt for the things they need. This is necessary for them to be able to live.

Track 33

1 Owls are divided into two groups, which are classified 'typical owls' and 'barn owls'.
2 Barn owls, which are nocturnal, fly silently.
3 Owls which are nomadic rear a great number of young.
4 Long-eared owls which live in the north migrate to Europe for winter.

Track 34

Hello everyone. As you know, this week's lectures are on wildlife in Britain, and today we're going to look at the barn owl, which is a common nocturnal creature around the British Isles. Now, if you have a look at page three of your handout, you will see an outline of a barn owl. Now, it looks like a harmless creature, but this actually couldn't be further from the truth. They may be relatively harmless to you and me, but to the British rodent, they are a killer! Now, why is this? Well, firstly it has a lot to do with their swiftness and silence. Look, for example, at the wings, which can vary from 80cm to 95cm. That's almost a metre! Wings that large have a great deal of power. Now, most people think that beaks are probably the way most birds hunt. But these beaks, which are curved downwards, are not used to hunt prey. When owls hunt prey, they have two massive anatomical advantages. Firstly, their feathers, which have serrated edges, can separate from each other. This makes their flight absolutely silent, so they can approach their prey unnoticed. It is their claws which are used to catch prey. Once they are upon the prey, the extremely powerful claws go into action. So, you'll see, they are not really as 'sweet' as they look! Now, their habitats...

Track 35

In this module, we're going to be exploring the natural habitats that the planet Earth provides, starting with probably one of the most famous, rainforests. Now, rainforests are exactly that: forests which see a great amount of rain. The reason they are so important is that they provide excellent conditions for many species to survive in. Let's look at how this is by exploring exactly what the rainforest is made up of.

Now, starting from the bottom of the rainforest, we can find the forest floor. Or rather we can't find it, as it is littered with leaves and branches which cover the ground! This area is a haven for creatures like spiders and all kinds of wildlife. Now, this forest floor occasionally has a shrub layer. This layer, which is only located near rivers, contains small trees and well, shrubbery, as the name suggests. It is a popular area for all manner of amphibians.

The next area within the rainforest is generally without light and extremely hot and damp. This area, which is called the understory, which by the way is all one word – under – story, is a popular home for creatures which dwell in the branches, like snakes, lizards, and sometimes even jaguars!

The most well-known area, called the canopy, is populated by some birds and small insects. The canopy is basically the tree-tops. It is the densely-packed canopy that blocks the light to the lower areas of rainforest. Not much reaches above the canopy, but there are a few exceptional trees that climb much further into the sky. These trees grow in areas called emergent zones. These zones, which are a perfect environment for birds and other small creatures, lie at the very top of the rainforest, and individual trees can stretch up to 50 metres in the air.

Now, as we can see, this means that rainforests have a multitude of unusual conditions, perfect for many creatures. But why are such conditions perfect? Well, let's go on to look....

Answer key

1 People and relationships

Exercise 1
1 shines *Tense:* Present simple
Rule number: 2
2 have you been *Tense:* Present perfect simple
Rule number: 3
3 does the bus leave *Tense:* Present simple
Rule number: 4
4 went/didn't like *Tense:* Past simple
Rule number: 2
5 has seen *Tense:* Present perfect simple
Rule number: 1
6 crossed *Tense:* Past simple
Rule number: 3

Exercise 2
1 has improved
2 disregarded
3 have invested
4 visit
5 partake
6 also had
7 include
8 brought
9 created
10 destroys

Exercise 3
1 do you live
2 come
3 have lived
4 moved
5 Do you
6 live
7 do
8 live
9 share
10 goes
11 Do you like
12 love
13 arrived
14 didn't like
15 have grown
16 know
17 have
18 has Moscow changed
19 has become
20 have opened
21 eat
22 have
23 came *OR* have come
24 meet

Exercise 4
Own answers

2 Free time

Exercise 1
1 have you been doing *Tense:* Present perfect continuous *Rule number:* 2
2 am watching *Tense:* Present continuous *Rule number:* 1
3 has been increasing *Tense:* Present perfect continuous *Rule number:* 1
4 was having *Tense:* Past continuous *Rule number:* 3
5 were walking *Tense:* Past continuous *Rule number:* 1
6 am reading *Tense:* Present continuous *Rule number:* 3

Exercise 2
1 I don't agree
2 I am having
3 I like
4 Do you mind
5 I'm thinking

Exercise 3
The amount of leisure time available to people <u>has been increasing</u> since the early twentieth century when machines started to be invented to do many labour intensive tasks both at work and in the home. Previously, people <u>were spending</u> many more hours doing basic menial tasks and as a result had less time available for hobbies and activities. Although recently many people <u>have been complaining</u> about their work life balance, studies show that the amount of free time we have <u>has been rising</u> continuously for over 50 years. More people <u>are playing</u> sport on a regular basis nowadays and young people <u>are taking up</u> traditional style hobbies such as knitting and walking in the countryside. There has also been a large amount of government investment in leisure facilities in local communities, which has assisted the uptake of hobbies for a range of people including children and the elderly. A few years ago, visitors to a local park would see people who <u>were playing</u> football or <u>walking</u> their dog. However, nowadays people <u>are using</u> the gym or a climbing wall as their way of sporting recreation.

Summary
1 has been increasing
2 are playing
3 are taking up

Exercise 4
a 1 has been rising
  2 are still buying
  (Note: *the number* + singular verb)
b 1 were viewing
  2 were watching

Exam practice model answer

This graph shows the kinds of activities done by old people in their spare time, covering a period from the 1980s to now in Europe. We can see that generally the activities listed have been increasing in popularity amongst the elderly, with hiking increasing steadily throughout the years, and playing sport being the most popular overall.

In the 1980s, nearly all activities were growing in popularity. The only activity which was becoming less popular over these years was going to the theatre. Going to the theatre declined steeply from 50% to 30%.

This changed in the 1990s, and going to the theatre became more popular, whereas reading saw a dramatic drop in popularity. The number of people doing all other activities increased.

This century, hiking, reading, going to the theatre and surfing the Internet have all been increasing in popularity. However, playing sport has been decreasing in popularity. Despite this, playing sport is still the second most popular activity nowadays amongst this group. Most elderly people are hiking nowadays in their spare time.
(*173 words*)
Note the tenses in both the continuous and simple.

3   Fame

Exercise 1
1 hadn't cared *Form:* past perfect
2 used to respect *Form:* used to
3 would dream *Form:* would
4 hadn't earned *Form:* past perfect
5 had always thought *Form:* past perfect
6 had been waiting *Form:* past perfect continuous

Exercise 2
1 had lived
2 had never travelled
3 used to work
4 'd been working
5 had travelled
6 had appeared

Exercise 3
Making money out of other people's fame is a highly specialized skill, but one that can bring great rewards to those who practise it proficiently. Marianne Beretoli is one of those people; she owns a company which sells information about celebrities to other celebrities as a kind of careers advice service. Although she was born in France, she use**d** to dream of moving to the USA, specifically Hollywood. Whilst studying business at university Beretoli was known for her innovative approach to applying theory to practice and she **would ~~to~~** often challenge the ideas of her tutors. When she had graduated, Beretoli worked in Paris and tried unsuccessfully to set up her own marketing agency. Then she decided to move to the USA and within months realised that she **had ~~been making~~ made** the right decision. She moved from Paris to Los Angeles in 1995 and after she had been working as an assistant for an advertising agency for a few years, she **~~had~~ set up** her own company providing information services to the rich and famous.

Exercise 4
1 B
2 C

Exam practice
1 A, C
2 b
3 b

4   Education

Exercise 1
1 'm going to *Form:* going to *Rule number:* 1
2 will *Form:* will *Rule number:* 3
3 's going to *Form:* going to *Rule number:* 2
4 won't *Form:* won't
5 will *Form:* will *Rule number:* 1

Exercise 2
1 C
2 A
3 B

Exercise 3
1 I'm going to walk
2 I'll call her
3 Shall I do it?

Exercise 4
Librarian:	Hello there. How can I help you?
John:	~~I will~~ **I'm going to** do a presentation on Mary Shelley, and I'd like to get some books on her.

Librarian:	Okay. The biographies are on the third floor. I'll ~~to~~ write the aisle number down for you.
John:	Thanks. I might use the Internet too and look for resources on there.
Librarian:	That's a good idea. If you're going **to** use the Internet, have a look on the Great British Authors website.
John:	Thanks, **I will** ~~I'm going to~~. I haven't heard of that site before. Thanks very much for the information.
Librarian:	That's quite all right. Feel free to come and ask me any questions and I ~~won't~~ **will** do my best to help.

Exam practice

1 D
2 B
3 A
4 C
5 C
6 A
7 A
8 B

5 The Internet

Exercise 1

1 'll be watching *Tense:* Future continuous *OR*
  'm watching *Tense:* Present continuous
2 will have moved *Tense:* Future perfect
3 'm changing *Tense:* Present continuous
4 will have become *Tense:* Future perfect simple
5 will have started *Tense:* Future perfect simple

Exercise 2

In the late 1990s experts predicted that online shopping would not be able to compete with in-store shopping yet the recent rise in online sales figures suggests that their predictions were wrong. In fact all evidence points to the fact that online shopping will have outstripped in-store shopping within the next five years. This rapid increase has been driven by a number of factors including price, convenience and choice. Most online retailers use a delivery service and as a result of tracking retailers shopping habits, many will soon be introducing specific delivery timings so that customers can ensure their goods are delivered when they are at home. Online companies are already working on innovative ways to attract customers. For example, later this year one of the country's largest electronics retailers, Browns, is launching a 24-hour replacement products service for customers who need to return faulty goods. Browns hopes that by 2015 over 90% of its customer base will have graduated to online purchasing.

As well as consumer goods another growth area is the travel industry. Travel experts estimate that in as little as five years' time travel agencies will have disappeared from our shopping centres and almost all travellers will be buying hotels and flights from online agencies.

Exercise 3

1 C
2 E
3 A
4 B
5 D

Exercise 4

1 over 50s
2 networked
3 Asia
4 (interactive) movies

Exercise 5

1 will have shifted
2 will have been playing
3 will have created
4 will have developed

Exam practice

1 first
2 10th – 31st
3 Social
4 digital map
5 July 22nd
6 tracking systems

6 The family

Exercise 1

1 The male was the main income earner in the last century.
2 Do you know whether extended families are traditional in Japan?
3 The government gives poorer families benefits.
4 Family members don't always get on well.
5 Household tasks are often shared by men and women.
6 Single parent families are becoming increasingly common in Western society.
7 There urgently need to be studies on why the family structure is less important.

Exercise 2

How important is the family?
It could be argued that the family is a structure in decline, yet many sociologists now claim that we are beginning to see a renewal in family values and family structures. Jason Lloyd, an eminent sociologist at the University of Salford, claims that today people are

yearning for the days of traditional family values. He asserts, " ...we can see examples of a renaissance of family values everywhere: in the TV adverts that sell products using happy families; in the promotions of seasonal family celebrations like Christmas; even in the language of politicians about social cohesion." Lloyd's claims have recently been echoed by other sociologists around the globe, which gives them even more weight. So, are we beginning to see a return to the traditional family structure? Only time will tell.

Exercise 3

I'm going to talk about my grandmother on my father's side. She is quite little and has white hair and glasses. I have glasses too. We are the only people in the family that wear glasses! She is very old now and I don't get to see her very often... I think I see her maybe two or three times a year. She lives quite far away in the countryside. It takes us about three hours to travel there. Whenever we visit, she always gives sweets to me. She is important to me because she is so kind and so nice, and I really love her. She is definitely my favourite family member! I think I take after her in some ways. We laugh at the same things and we both like reading. When we go and visit, we always go out walking in the fields and have a really lovely time. My dad always says that we are very similar. I would like to be as wise as her when I am older. I would also like to have a similar life. She had a very successful career. She was a doctor and worked for charities. She was very much in love with my grandfather, which I think is lovely.

Exercise 4

Adoption has long been a common thing, yet there has been a recent trend in adopting children from overseas. This trend has been noted in the media as more and more celebrities have adopted children from other countries. Some people think this is a negative thing, but I think that on the whole the positive effects of this outweigh any negative repercussions as I shall go on to show.

Firstly, adopting from other countries raises the awareness of a country's plight. Seeing famous people adopting children from countries like Cambodia means that Cambodia is in the news more and people can find out what is going on there. Also, these children move to richer countries and can tell people about their native country, raising awareness on a smaller scale.

Secondly, these children may well not be adopted unless people come from overseas to do it. A happy life in another country is surely better than an unhappy life in the country where a person was born. The new country will give the child more opportunity and a family that they may not get if they were to stay in the orphanage.

However, it is important for the children to retain their culture. There is a danger that this might not

happen if they move to another country. Therefore there should be a rule that the adoptive parents allow the child to revisit their home country and retain their original culture.

In conclusion, I think the personal benefits adoption gives a child and the awareness that can be raised from these adoptions far outweighs any negative factors, such as change of culture.

Exam practice model answer

Education comes from many places, not just formal schooling. People learn from their family, their friends, the television and personal experience among many other ways. Although these avenues of learning are certainly important, I believe that education within schools is much more important, as it lays the foundations for future achievement and wider success as I shall show.

Firstly, formal qualifications which are earned at school are often the entry points to certain careers and jobs. In order to be a lawyer or doctor, you need to do well at school so you can go on to study for professional qualifications. Additionally, many jobs ask for basic qualifications in maths and English when you apply. Without these qualifications, an individual could become limited in what they can do with their professional lives.

In addition to this, school also prepares you for relationships outside your family, which is an important aspect of life. School is a good socialisation tool because a student needs to deal with relationships on many different levels, for example with teachers and school friends, and they also need to deal with threats to happiness such as bullying or workloads.

Families are important as often children gain their moral outlook and aspirational goals from their parents. However, children can succeed without a favourable family setting to a certain extent. It is doubtful whether they could succeed without schooling.

In conclusion, although there are many beneficial forms of education, I believe schooling is more important than education within the family. This is because formal education gives you qualifications and socialisation that the family cannot offer.

7   The environment

Exercise 1

1 believe
2 are
3 has
4 changes
5 are
6 do

Exercise 2
1 c
2 a
3 d
4 b

Exercise 3
The graph **shows** the amount of wildlife in gardens in cities in the UK from 1980s to 2010s. Overall, the number of birds and insects **has** increased, whereas the number of butterflies has decreased. There were four million butterflies in UK city gardens in the 1980s however, **this** number decreased rapidly from 2000 to 2010 and now butterflies **are** the least populous of the three groups with only two million in UK city gardens. Both birds and insects have increased steadily in quantity over the period. The quantity of birds **has** increased from 2.5 to 3.5 million and insects **have** increased from 2.0 to 4.5 million. In general it can be said that each decade **has** seen a rise in bird and insect numbers.

Exercise 4
1 thinks
2 Some climatologists
3 is difficult
4 government and scientists

Exam practice
1 both
2 (deep sea) nets
3 an important factor
4 noise of ships
5 is useful

8 Food

Exercise 1
1 meat
2 few
3 soup
4 meats
5 a bowl of soup, some
6 much

Exercise 2
1 much meat
2 meals
3 sugar
4 juice or water
5 a couple of

Exercise 3
Last year I went to a wonderful restaurant overlooking the river in my city, Marseille, with a group of friends. The special occasion was my friend's 21st birthday and we decided to go out for dinner. We wanted to eat ~~a~~

beef because this restaurant is famous for meat, but as we arrived late they didn't have ~~many beefs~~ left. Instead we ate bouillabaisse which is a kind of seafood stew containing ~~a~~ **fish** and shellfish. I had a couple of glasses of orange juice. For dessert we each had **a slice of birthday cake~~s~~** which the restaurant had made especially for my friend. The cake had **21 candles** and my friend blew them all out in one go so she made ~~much~~ **a lot of** wishes for the future. We had so ~~many~~ **much** fun that night.

For Exam practice model answer see audio script Track 12.

9 Employment and finance

Exercise 1
1 the *Rule:* 1
2 a *Rule:* 1
3 – *Rules:* 1 and 2, – *Rule:* 1
4 – *Rule:* 3, the *Rule:* 5
5 – *Rule:* 2
6 an *Rule:* 4
7 the *Rule:* 3

Exercise 2
1 A
2 the
3 –
4 the
5 –
6 a
7 the
8 the
9 the
10 the
11 the
12 –
13 the
14 a
15 a
16 the
17 –
18 the
19 –
20 the

Exercise 3
1 the reasons
2 third
3 people are bored
4 difficult task
5 the family

Exercise 4

The pie chart shows the main careers of millionaires in the United States in percentages. We can see that ~~the~~ the majority of millionaires are businesspeople, while other jobs such as in ~~the~~ entertainment or ~~the~~ politics only represent **a** small proportion of the total. However, it could be said that millionaires are mostly people in the business and entertainment industries.

In the USA, people who work in ~~a~~ business account for just under two thirds of millionaires. **The** next largest group of millionaires on the chart is people who work in film and television. They account for 15% of the total. This group is closely followed by people who work in music. This sector accounts for **a** tenth of all millionaires in the USA.

The smaller groups all make up fewer than 10% of millionaires when combined. These people are sportspeople, politicians and people in other careers. The smallest group is **the** 'other' group with two per cent.

Exam practice model answer

The bar chart shows the percentage of people who have part-time jobs in the countries that make up the United Kingdom, both in 1980 and in 2010. There has generally been a small increase in part-time workers from 1980 to 2010, except in Northern Ireland. The graph also shows that England and Wales have far more part-time workers than Northern Ireland and Scotland.

In 1980, 25% of people in England worked part time. The only country with a greater percentage of part-time workers was Wales, with around 33% working part time. Both countries saw an increase in the percentage of people working part time in 2010. In England, the percentage rose to over 30% and in Wales percentage rose to just over 35%.

Scotland had the smallest percentage of part-time workers in 1980, with just over ten per cent. However, this rose to almost 20% in 2010 which is a large increase. Lastly, Northern Ireland was the only country which had a decreasing percentage of part-time workers. In 1980, it had around 15% of people in part-time work. This decreased by a couple of per cent in 2010.

10   Youth

Exercise 1

1 As a result *OR* Therefore *Function:* Result
2 In addition to *Function:* Addition
3 Thirdly, Lastly, Finally *Function:* Ordering
4 due to *OR* because of *Function:* Reason
5 but *OR* yet *Function:* Contrast
6 In conclusion *OR* In summary *Function:* Summarizing

Exercise 2

1 Volunteering
2 community based
3 expensive (to staff)
4 Drama
5 likely to continue
6 new schemes

Exercise 3

1 due to
2 for example
3 although
4 In addition to
5 However
6 because of
7 Lastly
8 such as
9 As a result of

Exercise 4

3 4 1 5 2 6 7

Exam practice

1 birth
2 embrace
3 unemployment
4 sub-norms
5 anti-social behaviour
6 (eventual) rejection

11   People and places

Exercise 1

1 D
2 S
3 D
4 D
5 S
6 D

Exercise 3

1 C
2 C
3 A

Exercise 4

1 The countryside hasn't become more attractive to families nowadays. *OR* The countryside has become less attractive to families nowadays. *OR* The city has become more attractive to families nowadays.
2 You've thought about the presentation a lot less clearly than me. *OR* You haven't thought about the presentation as clearly as me. *OR* I've thought about the presentation a lot more clearly than you.

3 We have done less research for the presentation than we could. *OR* We haven't done as much research for the presentation as we could.

4 Our final grade will be as high as our last presentation. *OR* Our final grade will be (much) higher than our last presentation.

Exam practice
1 B
2 C
3 B
4 C

12 Crime

Exercise 1
1 should go *OR* ought to go
2 have to follow *OR* must follow
3 might *OR* may *OR* could
4 don't have to pay a fine
5 can take

Exercise 2
1 might *OR* could *OR* may
2 might not *OR* may not
3 should
4 should *OR* ought to

Exercise 3
Crime prevention **musts** start from education. If people are not raised well, then they ~~will~~ **might/may/could** commit crimes in the future. It's the responsibility of both parents and schools to educate children in the difference between right and wrong. This could be done in special ethics classes in schools, and perhaps parenting classes **mightn't** be a good idea for parents who are unsure of how to raise children with more moral values. These classes shouldn't be compulsory though as this **might** ~~to~~ be too expensive and unnecessary. However, although all parents ~~mustn't~~ **might not** go, it could be useful for those who are struggling. More information ~~will~~ **might/may/could** help these parents.

For Exam practice model answers see audio script Track 20.

13 The Planet

Exercise 1
1 couldn't have known *OR* mustn't have known
2 had to hunt
3 should have taken *OR* ought to have taken
4 must have been
5 might/could/may have been inhabiting *OR* might/could/may have inhabited

6 could travel
7 didn't have to pay
8 must have been developing *OR* must have developed

Exercise 2
1 might have
2 had to
3 didn't have to
4 could
5 shouldn't have
6 couldn't have

Exercise 3
1 couldn't
2 could have *OR* might have
3 couldn't have
4 couldn't
5 should have *OR* ought to have
6 must have

Exercise 4
1 tree line
2 rainy
3 snow line
4 plant species
5 (dinosaur) fossils
6 scientific
7 4 weeks

Exam practice
1 narrow
2 Andrew
3 relevant information
4 much information
5 constantly moving

14 Globalization

Exercise 1
1 would not have gone, had not opened *Conditional:* third
2 buy, want *Conditional:* zero
3 continues, will stay *Conditional:* first
4 would not communicate, had developed *Conditional:* mixed (second + third)
5 were connected, would be *Conditional:* second

Exercise 2 Suggested answers
2 local businesses will continue to disappear.
3 the way we communicate could start to change in a negative way.
4 we will have a better world.

Exercise 4 Model answers
2 Student: I don't think so. If globalization <u>had caused</u> young people to care less about their countries, we <u>wouldn't see</u> so much national pride in sporting

competitions like The Olympics or the World Cup.
Conditional: third or mixed

3 Student: I would say that they should be more
positive. <u>If</u> globalization <u>didn't exist,</u> we <u>wouldn't
have</u> so many opportunities for work, travel and we
<u>wouldn't be able</u> to buy so many different products.
Conditional: first or second

4 Student: I think this depends on what
you mean by equal. <u>If</u> people in a country
<u>have</u> the same opportunities in life, then
globalization <u>is</u> good and can help the world
but this is not always what happens.
Conditional: any

**For Exam practice model answers see audio script
Track 26.**

15 Culture and modern society

Exercise 1
1 she had been to the opera the day
before and had really enjoyed it.
2 the government had to invest
more money in the arts.
3 the museum hadn't had any internationally
recognized exhibitions for several years.
4 what the theatre director intended
to do to increase ticket sales.
5 warned that
6 said *OR* claimed that
7 denied *OR* argued that
8 recommended

Exercise 3
1 had declined, was
2 had misrepresented
3 was not, attended
4 had, would *OR* have, will (if still true now)

Exam practice
1 True
2 Not given
3 True
4 False
5 Not given

16 Health and fitness

Exercise 1
1 your
2 their
3 It *OR* This
4 They *OR* These
5 it *OR* this

6 This *OR* That
7 He *OR* She, it
8 then

Exercise 2
1 your
2 their
3 my
4 theirs
5 These
6 you
7 this / that
8 It / This / That

Exercise 3
1 In my opinion politicians should listen to the
people that vote for ~~they~~ **them**. People want
to buy healthy food but it is expensive so they
buy fast food instead which is not good for ~~his~~
their health. Politicians should change ~~it~~ **this**
situation.
2 Dieticians suggest vitamins are necessary
to combat allergies. ~~It~~ **This** view has been
criticized by scientists who say that ~~this~~ **such/
these** nutrients do not always help to reduce
allergies. Therefore, because ~~them~~ **they** don't
agree, people don't know what advice to follow.
3 Organic food is not a solution to the health
problems of the world. ~~Its~~ **It** is less efficient
than other methods of food production. In
addition, ~~that~~ **these/those** problems are
more often related to less wealthy families
in developing countries. Families who live
~~then~~ **there** cannot afford to buy organic
produce so ~~they~~ **this** is not useful for us.

Exercise 4
1 supermarkets
2 fruit and vegetables have increased
considerably in price
3 a rise in obesity and other health related problems
4 my mother
5 (many) young people
6 the basic cooking skills
7 cooking
8 young people
9 processed meals
10 processed meals

Exam practice model essay

Healthcare costs all over the world are rising due
the rise in modern diseases which are a product of
unhealthy lifestyles. These lifestyles include poor diet,
smoking and lack of exercise. While many people do
not need to use medical services, there are others who
constantly need medication due to their unhealthy daily

lives. In my view people who are responsible for their own illness should have to contribute towards the cost of their medical treatment.

First of all, it is important to highlight the fact that ignorance is not an excuse. Information about health and fitness is widely available so everyone should know that smoking and eating fast food are not only bad for our health, but can cause serious diseases. Furthermore, there is a wide range of help services which people can consult for advice on improving their health from doctors to sports trainers and dieticians. People who continue to live unhealthy lifestyles despite advice from doctors or medical professional should not receive free or reduced cost medical services.

Secondly, it is clear that certain types of treatment are very expensive and some diseases can be prevented by adopting a healthy lifestyle. If people who are obese require treatment, they are taking money away from another patient, whose operation or treatment may be costly, but necessary. Therefore it could be a good solution to make people pay some money towards the cost of their treatment. If their health improved, this payment could be reduced.

In conclusion, making people contribute towards the cost of medical treatment for self-inflicted diseases could help reduce this type of disease and make more money available for other people.

(275 words)

17   Fashion

Exercise 1
1 D
2 B
3 E
4 C
5 A

Exercise 2
Paragraph 1, beginning *The bar chart...* = **B**
Paragraph 2, beginning *Overall...* = **A**
Paragraph 3, beginning *Regarding...* = **C**

Exercise 3
1 C
2 B
3 A

Exam practice
A vi
B viii
C ii
D i
E v

18   Film and entertainment

Exercise 1
1 To a certain extent, popular culture is being dictated by the entertainment industry.
2 The new Broadway play, *Star Memories*, should be avoided.
3 In the USA, cinema-going has been voted as the most popular weekend hobby.
4 The entertainment industry is known to be very competitive. *OR* It is known that the entertainment industry is very competitive.
5 Hollywood is regarded as the most influential town for filmmaking.
6 At the beginning of the 20th Century, famous actors and actresses were contractually restricted (by large film companies).
7 In relation to the plot of the book, the ending of the film had been changed.
8 We were told to sit in seats 4a and 4b.

Exercise 2
1 was founded
2 most well known
3 the standards
4 TV categories were
5 50th/fiftieth anniversary

Exercise 3
'My favourite book is called the *Hunger Games*. It was ~~wrote~~**written** by Suzanne Collins I think and it is a really good book. The story is set in North America, but at a time when things are very bad. It's a story of a terrible society, which **is** separated into districts. A boy and girl from each district ~~send~~ **are sent** to take part in the Hunger Games. These games are televised for everyone to see. The games are basically a fight to the death for the children taking part. The story follows a girl called Katniss, who **is** forced to take part in the games when she offers herself up instead of her sister. I like the story so much because it is very exciting. At first, I found it really horrifying, but the more I read it, the more I couldn't put the book down. I really came to like the main character too. She is so strong. I was **recommended** this book by some friends and it didn't disappoint me.'

Exercise 4
The student didn't talk about the main themes in the book.

For Exam practice model answers see audio script Track 31.

19 Wildlife

Exercise 1

1 The animal liberation league, whose opinion was criticized by senior politicians, failed... (non-defining)
2 Wildlife in Mexico, which has flourished for many years, is now.... (non-defining)
3 which OR that (defining)
4 Dian Fossey, who died in 1985, helped...(non-defining)
5 London, where a third of the city is actually open space, is home... (non-defining)
6 which OR that (defining)
7 which OR that (defining)
8 Evolution, which is the generally accepted theory of how life on earth developed, is... (non-defining)

Sentence 7 can have the relative pronoun omitted.

Exercise 2

1 that keep animals in small cages
2 that give the animals space to move and look after them well
3 that have no laws to protect their animals
4 which have been destroyed by industries
5 , which are one of the most endangered rainforest species,
6 , when the main purpose is enjoyment,
7 which don't have shops to buy food

Exercise 3

1 ...two groups, which... (non-defining)
2 ...owls, which are nocturnal, fly... (non-defining)
3 (defining – there are resident owls which produce only 2 offspring)
4 (defining – there are southern long-eared owls which do not migrate)

Exercise 4

1 Wings
2 to hunt prey
3 (can) separate
4 catch prey

Exam practice

1 leaves and branches
2 near rivers
3 Understory
4 (perfect) environment for

20 Men and women

Exercise 1

1 A large audience of dedicated fans = determiner + adjective + noun + prepositional phrase

2 The politician who had proposed new laws on paternity rights = determiner + noun + relative clause
3 The development of language skills in boys and girls = determiner + general noun + specific noun + prepositional phrase
4 The latest figures from the Driving Standards Agency = determiner + adjective + noun + prepositional phrase
5 Gender intelligence stereotypes = noun + noun + noun
6 Men who decide to give up work to bring up their children = noun + relative clause

Exercise 2

1 a large quantity of household products that we use in our daily lives
2 a language for programming computers
3 the scientific and technical education of women
4 a dramatic rise in the number of women who are studying and working in science and technology
5 the importance of a focused education which allows people to develop their skills

Exercise 3 Suggested answers

2 the range/type of activities for boys and girls
3 the availability/amount of space for physical exercise
4 the amount/number of children in a class OR the size of classes
5 the personality/character of the teacher
6 the sum/amount of money spent on facilities

Exercise 4 model answer

Some people argue that the types of jobs which are more suited to men are in more technical fields such as engineering or construction. However, this is not always true as can be seen in the increase in female engineers over recent decades. The range of employment opportunities for men and women has changed dramatically over the last twenty years. Nowadays, for example, the skills needed for working in business are taught at school and university and women are just as capable as men in acquiring these skills. In fact, women who hold senior positions in business are excellent role models for both girls and boys.

Exam practice model answer

Although the care of children has traditionally been the role of women, nowadays many men have decided to stay at home to raise children while the woman in the family goes to work. However, some people believe that women have a natural ability for childcare and this role should be left to them. I disagree with this for the following reasons.

Firstly, both men and women have qualities which are important for bringing up and educating children. These qualities are not specific to men or women, therefore both genders are able to raise children successfully. By saying that childcare is a specific female role, children will receive a message which portrays women as carers only. For example, young girls who are taught to believe that the place of women is in the home may not try hard in school subjects which are more male dominated, such as science.

Secondly, the role of women in the workplace has changed significantly in the last fifty years. Many women now hold senior positions in many areas of employment. Women contribute a range of skills to the workplace which are both valuable and important. In my opinion, women should continue to focus on their careers and ensure that their daughters are aware of the opportunities which are available to them in life. Men should also take on some of the responsibility of childcare and teach their sons that this is a valuable role in society for men as well as women.

In conclusion, it is important that men and women share childcare duties because both genders have important qualities and skills. However, women and men should also be allowed to focus on their careers and provide strong role models for children.

(*287 words*)

Grammar reference

Unit 1   Simple tenses

Present simple – subject + present verb

+	-	?
I live	I don't live	do I live?
he/she/it lives	he/she/it doesn't live	does he/she/it live?
we live	we don't live	do we live?
you live	you don't live	do you live?
they live	they don't live	do they live?

Past simple – subject + past verb

+	-	?
I lived	I didn't live	did I live?
he/she/it lived	he/she/it didn't live	did he/she/it live?
we lived	we didn't live	did we live?
you lived	you didn't live	did you live?
they lived	they didn't live	did they live?

Present perfect – subject + *has/have* + past participle

+	-	?
I have lived	I haven't lived	have I lived?
he/she/it has lived	he/she/it hasn't lived	has he/she/it lived?
we have lived	we haven't lived	have we lived?
you have lived	you haven't lived	have you lived?
they have lived	they haven't lived	have they lived?

Unit 2   Continuous tenses

Present continuous – subject + *to be* + (verb)*ing*

+	-	?
I am watching	I'm not watching	am I watching?
he/she/it is watching	he/she/it isn't watching	is he/she/it watching?
we are watching	we aren't watching	are we watching?
you are watching	you aren't watching	are you watching?
they are watching	they aren't watching	are they watching?

Present continuous – subject + *was/were* + (verb)*ing*

+	-	?
I was watching	I wasn't watching	was I watching?
he/she/it was watching	he/she/it wasn't watching	was he/she/it watching?
we were watching	we weren't watching	were we watching?
you were watching	you weren't watching	were you watching?
they were watching	they weren't watching	were they watching?

Present Perfect Continuous – Subject + *has/have* + *been* + (verb)*ing*

+	-	?
I have been watching	I haven't been watching	have I been watching?
he/she/it has been watching	he/she/it hasn't been watching	has he/she/it been watching?
we have been watching	we haven't been watching	have we been watching?
you have been watching	you haven't been watching	have you been watching?
they have been watching	they haven't been watching	have they been watching?

Unit 3   Past

Past perfect – subject + *had* + past participle

+	-	?
I had played	I hadn't played	had I played?
he/she/it had played	he/she/it hadn't played	had he/she/it played?
we had played	we hadn't played	had we played?
you had played	you hadn't played	had you played?
they had played	they hadn't played	had they played?

Past perfect continuous – subject + *had* + *been* + (verb)*ing*

+	-	?
I had been playing	I hadn't been playing	had I been playing?
he/she/it had been playing	he/she/it hadn't been playing	had he/she/it been playing?
we had been playing	we hadn't been playing	had we been playing?
you had been playing	you weren't playing	had you been playing?
they had been playing	they weren't playing	had they been playing?

Used to – subject + *used to* + verb

+	-	?
I used to play	I didn't use to play	did I use to play?
he/she/it used to play	he/she/it didn't use to play	did he/she/it use to play?
we used to play	we didn't use to play	did we use to play?
you used to play	you didn't use to play	did you use to play?
they used to play	they didn't use to play	did they use to play?

Would – subject + *would* + verb

+
I would play
he/she/it would play
we would play
you would play
they would play

Unit 4   Future 1

Going to – Subject + *to be* + *going to* + infinitive

+	-	?
I am going to learn	I'm not going to learn	am I going to learn?
he/she/it is going to learn	he/she/it isn't going to learn	is he/she/it going to learn?
we are going to learn	we aren't going to learn	are we going to learn?
you are going to learn	you aren't going to learn	are you going to learn?
they are going to learn	they aren't going to learn	are they going to learn?

Will – Subject + *will* + infinitive

+	-	?
I will learn	I won't learn	will/shall I learn?
he/she/it will learn	he/she/it won't learn	will he/she/it learn?
we will learn	we won't learn	will/shall we learn?
you will learn	you won't learn	will you learn?
they will learn	they won't learn	will they learn?

Unit 5   Future 2

Future continuous – subject + *will* + *be* + (verb)*ing*

+	-	?
I will be waiting	I won't be waiting	will/shall I be waiting?
he/she/it will be waiting	he/she/it won't be waiting	will he/she/it be waiting?
we will be waiting	we won't be waiting	will/shall we be waiting?
you will be waiting	you won't be waiting	will you be waiting?
they will be waiting	they won't be waiting	will they be waiting?

Future perfect simple – subject + *will* + *have* + past participle

+	-	?
I will have waited	I won't have waited	will/shall I have waited?
he/she/it will have waited	he/she/it won't have waited	will he/she/it have waited?
we will have waited	we won't have waited	will/shall we have waited?
you will have waited	you won't have waited	will you have waited?
they will have waited	they won't have waited	will they have waited?

Future perfect continuous – subject + *will* + *have* + *been* + past participle

+	-	?
I will have been waiting	I won't have been waiting	will/shall I have been waiting?
he/she/it will have been waiting	he/she/it won't have been waiting	will he/she/it have been waiting?
we will have been waiting	we won't have been waiting	will/shall we have been waiting?
you will have been waiting	you won't have been waiting	will you have been waiting?
they will have been waiting	they won't have been waiting	will they have been waiting?

Unit 11   Comparatives and superlatives

Comparative and superlative adjectives

adjective	comparative	superlative
small (ends in double consonant)	smaller (+er)	the smallest
big (ends in consonant + vowel + consonant)	bigger (+ final consonant + er)	the biggest
late (ends in e)	later (+ r)	the latest
early (ends in y)	earlier (y + i + er)	the earliest

Irregular comparative and superlative adjectives

adjective	comparative	superlative
good	better	best
bad	worse	worst
far	farther/further	the farthest/furthest
old	older/elder	the oldest/eldest

Comparative and superlative adverbs

adverb	comparative	superlative
fast (same form as adjective)	faster (+ er)	the fastest (+ est)
quietly (adjective + ly)	more quietly (+ more)	the most quietly (+ the most)

Irregular comparative and superlative adverbs

adverb	comparative	superlative
well	better	best
badly	worse	worst
far	farther/ further	the farthest/furthest

Unit 14   Conditionals

Zero conditional

if/ when + present simple + present simple

Other possible structures:

If + modal verb + modal verb

+	-	?
If/when people have free time, they enjoy life.	If/when people don't have free time, they do not enjoy life.	If/when people have free time, do they enjoy life?

First conditional

if + present simple + *will* + infinitive without '*to*'

Other possible structures:

if + present simple + *can/could/may/might*
if + present simple + imperative
if + present continuous + *will* + infinitive without '*to*'
if + present perfect + *will* + infinitive without '*to*'

+	-	?
If people have free time, they will enjoy life.	If people don't have free time, they won't enjoy life.	If people have free time, will they enjoy life?

Second conditional

if + past simple + *would* + infinitive without '*to*'

Other possible structures:

if + past simple + *could/might*
if + *were to* + *would* + infinitive without '*to*'
if + past simple + *should* + infinitive without '*to*'

+	-	?
If people had free time, they would enjoy life.	If people didn't have free time, they wouldn't enjoy life.	If people had free time, would they enjoy life?

Third conditional

if + past perfect simple + *would have* + past participle

Other possible structures:

if + past perfect simple + *could/might*
if + *were to* + *would* + infinitive without '*to*'
if + past simple + *should* + infinitive without '*to*'

+	-	?
If people had had free time, they would have enjoyed life.	*If people hadn't had free time, they wouldn't have enjoyed life.*	*If people had had free time, would they have enjoyed life?*

Mixed conditional

if + past perfect simple + *would* + infinitive without '*to*'
if + past simple + *would have* + past participle

+	-	?
If people had had free time, they would enjoy life.	*If people hadn't had free time, they wouldn't enjoy life.*	*If people hadn't had free time, would they enjoy life?*
If people had free time, they would have enjoyed life.	*If people didn't have free time, they would enjoy life.*	*If people had free time, would they have enjoyed life?*

Unit 15   Reported Speech

Tense changes

Direct speech	Reported/indirect speech
Present simple: 'I _like_ opera'	Past simple: She said (that) she _liked_ opera.
Present simple continuous: 'I'_m studying_ Japanese flower arranging.'	Past continuous: He said (that) he _was studying_ Japanese flower arranging.
Present perfect simple: 'I _have never been_ to the National Museum.'	Past perfect: He said (that) he _had never been_ to the National Museum.
Present perfect continuous: 'We'_ve been painting_ for many years.'	Past perfect continuous: He said (that) they _had been painting_ for many years.
Past simple: 'We _went_ to the theatre.'	Past perfect: He said (that) they _had gone_ to the theatre.
Past continuous: 'Yesterday I _was listening_ to the lecture on the radio show.'	Past perfect continuous: She said that the previous day she _had been listening_ to the lecture on the radio show.
Past perfect: 'I _had read_ the novel.'	Past perfect: She said (that) she _had read_ the novel.
Going to (present): 'I'_m going to visit_ the local craft shop.'	Going to (past): She said (that) she _was going to visit_ the local craft shop.'
Will: 'I'_ll_ start photography classes soon.'	Would: He said (that) he _would_ start photography classes soon.
Can: 'I _can_ draw well.'	Could: She said (that) she _could_ draw well.
May: 'I think young people _may_ not be interested in reading.'	Might: The teacher said she thought (that) young people _might_ not be interested in reading.
Must: 'I _must_ attend my son's school orchestra concert.'	Had to: My boss said (that) he _had to_ attend his son's school orchestra concert.

Time/place word changes

today → _that day_

tomorrow → _the next/following day_

yesterday → _the day before/the previous day_

3 days ago → _3 days before/earlier_

now → _then_

here → _there_

Unit 18   Passive Constructions

The passive can only be used with a verb that takes an object.

Present simple	*am/is/are* + past participle
Present continuous	*am/is/are* + *being* + past participle
Past simple	*was/were* + past participle
Past continuous	*was/were* + *being* + past participle
Present perfect	*have/has* + *been* + past participle
Present perfect continuous (unusual)	*have/has* + *been* + *being* + past participle
Past perfect	*had* + *been* + past participle
Past perfect continuous (unusual)	*had* + *been* + *being* + past participle
Used to	*used to* + *be* + past participle
Would	*would* + *be* + past participle
Will	*will* + *be* + past participle
Going to	*is/are* + *going to* + *be* + past participle
Modal constructions – present/future	e.g. *should* + *be* + past participle
Modal constructions – past	e.g. *should have* + *been* + past participle
Semi-modal constructions	e.g. *had to* + *be* + past participle

Other Passive Constructions (avoiding using the subject)

A common way to use most reporting verbs in the passive is:
to be + past participle of the reporting verb + *to* + past participle

> **Active:**   *People say that films distort real life.*
> **Passive:** *Films are said to distort real life.*

> **Active:**   *They advise parents to monitor the programmes their children watch.*
> **Passive:** *Parents are advised to monitor the programmes their children watch.*

Some verbs (e.g. say, know, believe, understand, find) can also be used in the following structure:
It is/was/has been + past participle of the reporting verb + *that* + clause

> **Active:**   *People say that films distort real life.*
> **Passive:** *It is said that films distort real life.*

> **Active:**   *Researchers have found that too many hours watching television can be detrimental.*
> **Passive:** *It has been found that too many hours watching television can be detrimental.*

The International English Language Testing System (IELTS) Test

IELTS is jointly managed by the British Council, Cambridge ESOL Examinations and IDP Education, Australia.

There are two versions of the test:

- Academic
- General Training

Academic is for students wishing to study at undergraduate or postgraduate levels in an English-medium environment.

General Training is for people who wish to migrate to an English-speaking country.

This book is primarily for students taking the Academic version.

The Test

There are four modules:

Listening	30 minutes, plus 10 minutes for transferring answers to the answer sheet NB: the audio is heard *only once*. Approx. 10 questions per section Section 1: two speakers discuss a social situation Section 2: one speaker talks about a non-academic topic Section 3: up to four speakers discuss an educational project Section 4: one speaker gives a talk of general academic interest
Reading	60 minutes 3 texts, taken from authentic sources, on general, academic topics. They may contain diagrams, charts, etc. 40 questions: may include multiple choice, sentence completion, completing a diagram, graph or chart, choosing headings, yes/no, true/false questions, classification and matching exercises.
Writing	Task 1: 20 minutes: description of a table, chart, graph or diagram (150 words minimum) Task 2: 40 minutes: an essay in response to an argument or problem (250 words minimum)
Speaking	11–14 minutes A three-part face-to-face oral interview with an examiner. The interview is recorded. Part 1: introductions and general questions (4–5 mins) Part 2: individual long turn (3–4 mins) – the candidate is given a task, has one minute to prepare, then talks for 1–2 minutes, with some questions from the examiner. Part 3: two-way discussion (4–5 mins): the examiner asks further questions on the topic from Part 2, and gives the candidate the opportunity to discuss more abstract issues or ideas.
Timetabling	Listening, Reading and Writing must be taken on the same day, and in the order listed above. Speaking can be taken up to 7 days before or after the other modules.
Scoring	Each section is given a band score. The average of the four scores produces the Overall Band Score. You do not pass or fail IELTS; you receive a score.

IELTS and the Common European Framework of Reference

The CEFR shows the level of the learner and is used for many English as a Foreign Language examinations. The table below shows the approximate CEFR level and the equivalent IELTS Overall Band Score:

CEFR description	CEFR code	IELTS Band Score
Proficient user	C2	9
(Advanced)	C1	7–8
Independent user	B2	5–6.5
(Intermediate – Upper Intermediate)	B1	4–5

This table contains the general descriptors for the band scores 1–9:

IELTS Band Scores		
9	Expert user	Has fully operational command of the language: appropriate, accurate and fluent with complete understanding.
8	Very good user	Has fully operational command of the language, with only occasional unsystematic inaccuracies and inappropriacies. Misunderstandings may occur in unfamiliar situations. Handles complex detailed argumentation well.
7	Good user	Has operational command of the language, though with occasional inaccuracies, inappropriacies and misunderstandings in some situations. Generally handles complex language well and understands detailed reasoning.
6	Competent user	Has generally effective command of the language despite some inaccuracies, inappropriacies and misunderstandings. Can use and understand fairly complex language, particularly in familiar situations.
5	Modest user	Has partial command of the language, coping with overall meaning in most situations, though is likely to make many mistakes. Should be able to handle basic communication in own field.
4	Limited user	Basic competence is limited to familiar situations. Has frequent problems in understanding and expression. Is not able to use complex language.
3	Extremely limited user	Conveys and understands only general meaning in very familiar situations. Frequent breakdowns in communication occur.
2	Intermittent user	No real communication is possible except for the most basic information using isolated words or short formulae in familiar situations and to meet immediate needs. Has great difficulty understanding spoken and written English.
1	Non user	Essentially has no ability to use the language beyond possibly a few isolated words.
0	Did not attempt the test	No assessable information provided.

Marking

The Listening and Reading papers have 40 items, each worth one mark if correctly answered. Here are some examples of how marks are translated into band scores:

Listening:
16 out of 40 correct answers:	band score 5
23 out of 40 correct answers:	band score 6
30 out of 40 correct answers:	band score 7

Reading
15 out of 40 correct answers:	band score 5
23 out of 40 correct answers:	band score 6
30 out of 40 correct answers:	band score 7

Writing and Speaking are marked according to performance descriptors.
Writing: examiners award a band score for each of four areas with equal weighting:

- Task achievement (Task 1)
- Task response (Task 2)
- Coherence and cohesion
- Lexical resource and grammatical range and accuracy

Speaking: examiners award a band score for each of four areas with equal weighting:

- Fluency and coherence
- Lexical resource
- Grammatical range
- Accuracy and pronunciation

For full details of how the examination is scored and marked, go to: www.ielts.org